The Insider's Guide to Santa Fe

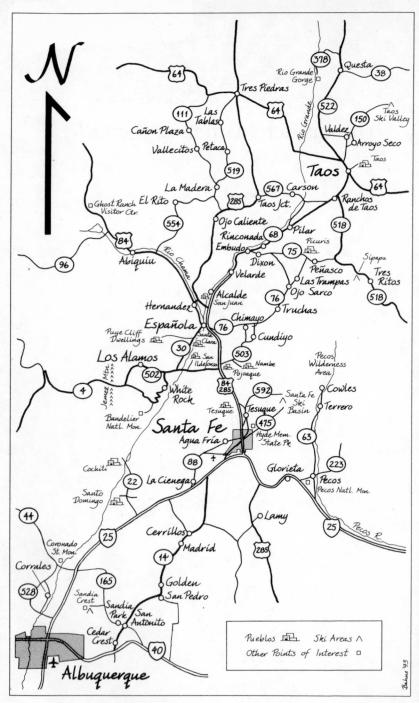

Santa Fe and Northern New Mexico

The Insider's Guide
to
SANTA FE

Third Revised Edition

Bill Jamison
and
Cheryl Alters Jamison

THE HARVARD COMMON PRESS
Boston, Massachusetts

The Harvard Common Press
535 Albany Street
Boston, Massachusetts 02118

Printed in the United States of America

LIBRARY OF CONGRESS CATALOGING-IN-PUBLICATION DATA
Jamison, Bill.
    The insider's guide to Santa Fe / Bill Jamison and
Cheryl Alters Jamison. — 3rd rev. ed.
      p.   cm.
    Includes index.
    ISBN 1-55832-056-3 : $9.95
    1. Santa Fe (N.M.)—Guidebooks. 2. Santa Fe Region
(N.M.)—Guidebooks. I. Jamison, Cheryl Alters. II. Title.
F804.S23J348 1993
917.89'560453—dc20   92-47250

Maps by Charles Bahne
Cover design by Jackie Schuman
Interior design by Linda Ziedrich

10 9 8 7 6 5 4 3 2 1

For Heather

Contents

Maps

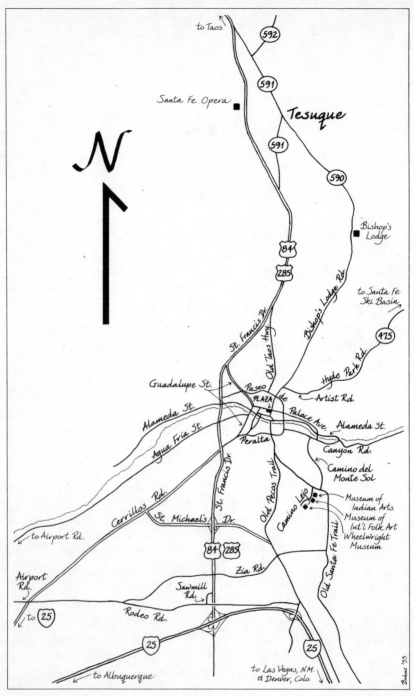

Santa Fe

Introduction
♦♦♦♦♦♦♦♦♦♦♦

Dancing Ground of the Sun

THE PUEBLO Indians established a village on the site of Santa Fe six or seven centuries ago, long before any Europeans arrived in the area. According to legend, they called the village "the dancing ground of the sun," a splendid description of the city's natural setting.

Though Santa Fe is small—about sixty thousand in population today—its natural surroundings are immense. If you approach the city from the south, as most visitors have for four hundred years, the vast Southwestern desert gradually and reluctantly yields to the forested peaks of the Jemez Mountains on the west and the Sangre de Cristo Mountains on the east. Interstate 25 from the Albuquerque airport, the entry route for most modern travelers, follows the valley of the Rio Grande between the mountains, parallel to the old Spanish route from Mexico City. The founders built the town along a mountain stream, the Santa Fe River, on a 7,000-foot plateau situated right under the towering shelter of the eastern range.

On the plateau the expansive sky overhead dominates the perspective. The desert below, like a great ocean, takes an infinity to reach the horizon. The mountains above, and those beyond in all directions, rise proudly and primordially over the arid land, daunting in their massiveness and seeming indifference. The Spanish wanted the view from the town primarily for protection against invaders, but it couldn't have escaped the notice of their priests that the sin of human pride would be hard to maintain in such a setting.

Many writers have strained for language that would match the grandeur of the scenery. D. H. Lawrence, who lived north of Santa Fe, near Taos, made one of the noblest efforts in the 1920s.

> For greatness of beauty I have never experienced anything like New Mexico. All those mornings when I went with a hoe along the ditch to the Cañón, at the ranch, and stood, in the fierce, proud silence of the Rockies, on their foothills, to look far over the desert to the blue mountains away in Arizona, blue as Chalcedony, with the sage-brush desert sweeping grey-blue in between, dotted with tiny cube-crystals of houses, the vast amphitheater of lofty, indomitable desert, sweeping round to the ponderous Sangre de Cristo Mountains on the east, and coming up flush at the pine-dotted foothills of the Rockies! What splendour!*

The land is a magnificent stage for the dazzling performance of the sun. When Lawrence tried to describe the place of the sun in the local environment, he stretched even further for an apt image.

> Never is the light more pure and overweening as there, arching with a royalty almost cruel over the hollow, uptilted world. It is so easy to understand

---

* The D. H. Lawrence quotes are from *Phoenix: The Posthumous Papers* (Penguin, 1936).

that the Aztecs gave hearts of men to the sun. For the sun is not merely hot or scorching, not at all. It is of a brilliant and unchallengeable purity and haughty serenity which would make one sacrifice the heart to it. Ah, yes, in New Mexico the heart is sacrificed to the sun and the human being is left stark, heartless, but undauntedly religious.

The sun's intensity in the area is due to a combination of circumstances. Its warmth results from Santa Fe's southern latitude, about the same as Atlanta's. Winter days are milder for skiing than anywhere else in the Rockies, though ski vests and sweaters remain useful all year, even on summer evenings, because of the contrasting coolness of the mountain air.

The sun's brightness comes from the clarity of the air. At Santa Fe's altitude its rays avoid the last mile and a half of the earth's dust-laden atmosphere. The desert aridity keeps the humidity low and the air relatively free of the misting effect of water particles. The size of the town and its lack of industry preclude serious air pollution. These factors combine to give the sun more rein than it has anywhere else in the United States.

It's the play of the sun and its shadow on mountain, desert and adobe that has lured so many artists to the area. Robert Henri and Marsden Hartley, who spent months in Santa Fe on several different visits, were fascinated with the brilliance of the color. Hartley said the area "is of course the only place in America where true color exists, excepting the short autumnal season in New England."

John Sloan, a leading figure in the "ashcan school" of American art, made a summer home where there were no ashcans, just off Canyon Road. His subject matter shifted to the local population, but what was most notable in his work was the shimmering glow of the sun. Andrew Dasburg, probably the greatest of the American cubists, moved permanently to New Mexico, first to Santa Fe and then to Taos. Dasburg said, "I felt as though I had come upon the Garden of Eden; everything was pristine."

The first people to appreciate the amplitude of the place, long before the artists arrived, were those who called it "the dancing ground of the sun." In the complex pantheistic beliefs of the Pueblo peoples, their natural surroundings assume sacred dimensions. Everything, animate and inanimate, has a spirit, which is benevolent or malevolent depending on how well humans respect it.

Most settlers who succeeded the Pueblos were less concerned about maintaining religious harmony with the environment than with using it. The Spanish wanted the mountains to yield gold, and the Americans looked to them for furs, coal, timber and now uranium. But most residents, and visitors, too, have felt something of the spiritual power that the Pueblos attribute to their land. D. H. Lawrence is not a very representative case for much of anything, but many new arrivals do share his first impression of the place. He came to the area after years of traveling the world, jaded by the expectation of monotony.

Superficially, the world has become small and known. Poor little globe of earth, the tourists trot round you as easily as they trot round the Bois or round Central Park. There is no mystery left, we've been there, we've seen it, we know all about it.

We are mistaken. I realized this with shattering force when I went to New Mexico. The moment I saw the brilliant, proud morning shine high up over the deserts of Santa Fe, something stood still in my soul and I started to attend. In the magnificent fierce morning of New Mexico one sprang awake, a new part of the soul woke up suddenly, and the old world gave way to a new.

PART ONE

♦ ♦ ♦ ♦ ♦ ♦ ♦ ♦ ♦

THE
SANTA FE
HERITAGE

Chapter One
♦♦♦♦♦♦♦♦♦♦♦

The Pueblos

THE ANCESTORS of the Pueblos, the Anasazi people, settled in the Southwest several thousand years
ago, but no one is certain of their origins. The Pueblo
explanation is the most interesting. They believe their
ancestors came from an underworld beneath the earth's
surface, a place that was dark, ugly and damp, the very
opposite of the Southwest. They struggled to climb out
and, after many vicissitudes, finally emerged through the
earth's navel, onto the land and into the light. The point
of emergence is represented by the small opening, or *si-
papu*, in Pueblo *kivas*, their sacred ceremonial chambers.

The Anasazi were nomadic hunters and gatherers until
they began cultivating corn, about 2000 B.C. Archaeolo-
gists have unearthed hundreds of tiny cobs from that
ancient period, as thin as pencils and less than two inches
in length. Over the next millennium the Anasazi refined
their agricultural methods, added the protein of the bean
to their repertory and learned how to support cities from
their farms. In their first permanent settlements they lived
in pit houses, large holes in the ground covered with

logs. The Anasazi developed these circular, underground structures originally as granaries for storing corn, but later found them suitable for housing as well.

The Pueblos have never forgotten the importance of corn in the development of their civilization. They use cornmeal and corn pollen as Catholics use holy water, to bless the newborn and the dead and to prepare for important rituals, and they celebrate its spiritual power in some of their most striking ceremonial dances. Their underground kivas have remained very similar in structure to the original corn granaries, long after their ancestors began building houses above ground.

The Anasazi were impressive architects. After leaving their pit houses, about the time that Europe was entering the Dark Ages, they constructed some magnificent cities. One of the oldest was in Chaco Canyon, a dry, hot valley in the desert canyonlands of northwestern New Mexico. In their prime, in the twelfth century, the Chaco residents built eight large stone structures capable of housing at least five thousand people. Pueblo Bonito, the grandest of these communal dwellings, was four stories high and contained eight hundred rooms and 30 kivas. It was the largest housing structure built in the Western Hemisphere until a New York City landlord topped it in the 1880s. The 40-foot-high walls, some of which are still standing, had to be massive at the base to support the building, but the Anasazi laid the stones with delicate and intricate artistry—as effectively as any mason could today with much more sophisticated tools.

Life in Chaco Canyon was probably as pleasant as possible for the Stone Age. The residents had an elaborate naturalistic religion that entailed frequent and splendid community ceremonies. They engaged in trade that ranged as far as the Pacific Ocean and brought them, among other things, various shells and gems for jewelry. The Anasazi knew basket weaving before coming to

Chaco and developed pottery after they settled in the canyon. They wove cotton blankets and colored them with vegetable dyes. Some of their possessions were so precious to them that they hid them in cleverly concealed wall crypts that have been discovered only by chance.

The Anasazi left Chaco for unknown reasons, possibly drought, during the thirteenth century. Most residents moved east to the Pajarito Plateau, overlooking the Rio Grande Valley. The major settlement, among many, on the 8,000-foot plateau was in Frijoles Canyon, an excellent home site. Six miles long and a half mile wide, the canyon is crossed by a small, spring-fed stream that carries ample water to irrigate the valley floor. Berries grow wild along the creek, and tall pines, good for lumber, cover the canyon's southern slope. The sheer north wall is dotted with natural caves, which some of the residents dug out and walled in for homes. Other people lived in a circular communal structure, three stories high, near the creek.

The ruins of the settlement are now a part of Bandelier National Monument, named for Adolph Bandelier, the first archaeologist to study the Pueblos. In a novel about the Frijoles people, *The Delight Makers* (Harcourt Brace Jovanovich, 1971), Bandelier speculated that they left the canyon largely because of feuds and witchcraft within the community.

By the time the Spanish arrived in the area in 1540, most of these natives had moved down from the Pajarito Plateau into their present villages along the Rio Grande Valley. Today there are 16 Pueblo communities in the valley, in an area stretching about 75 miles both north and south of Santa Fe. The other three Pueblo villages in New Mexico, and the Hopi villages in Arizona, are west of the valley.

The Spanish named the people of all of these towns *Pueblo,* meaning "community" or "village," because of their settled life. Actually each community, or *pueblo,* is a separate tribal group, with its own traditions and local laws. The people share a common cultural background and are still known generically as Pueblos, but they speak six different languages, varying considerably in some cases even among villages in close proximity.

In many respects life in the present pueblos is very similar to what the Spanish encountered more than four centuries ago. The Spanish, and later the Americans, tried to introduce changes in Pueblo life, and did succeed to some degree, but on the whole ancient Pueblo traditions have prevailed. The extent of change varies substantially from one community to another, since each is fully independent and self-governing, but generally the Pueblos have accepted things they found useful and rejected anything that seemed likely to destroy the continuity of their way of life.

In government, the various villages have each retained the ancient form of council rule. The Spanish forced the Pueblos to choose a governor for each community, to act as a spokesman and liaison to the outside world, but important decisions are still made by a council of experienced leaders representing the most significant interests in the pueblo. In council, now as in the past, unanimity is the goal in reaching decisions, even when this requires holding interminable meetings or leaving an important matter unresolved for a considerable time. Religious leaders, caciques, are still influential in decisions, though they do not dominate councils as they did in the past.

Both the Spanish and the Americans attempted to eliminate the native religion. The Spanish tried diligently to convert the Pueblos to Catholicism, and later the Americans arbitrarily assigned all Indians to various Christian churches. One Baptist missionary sent to Laguna Pueblo was so zealous in his efforts that he caused a major split in the village that has never fully healed. The Spanish, who were usually more patient and persistent, were slightly more successful.

Most of the Pueblos accepted Catholicism to the degree that it did not interfere with their own ancient beliefs. Saints were easy to adopt because they were similar in some respects to the various Pueblo deities, the *kachinas*. Prayer and mass were sensible to the Pueblos, analogous to their own rituals, and the Christian calendar offered a few refinements over their own in tracking the important changes in the seasons. Other Christian concepts were more often tolerated than endorsed.

When the Pueblos adopted elements of Christianity, they regarded them as a supplement to their existing religion, not as a replacement. At first this was very frustrating to the Spanish, but they learned over time that efforts to suppress the old beliefs could be even more frustrating. The peaceful Pueblos killed overly righteous priests, and in one instance organized the most effective mass routing the Spanish empire ever encountered in the New World in response to an attempt to quash their religion. Eventually the two peoples reached a compromise. The Spanish began looking the other way and the Pueblos went underground—literally—with their religion. They banned the Spanish, and later the Americans, from their kivas, where they continued their most sacred ancient rites in seclusion.

In more ordinary and practical matters, the Pueblos have been less resistant to change. They have traded housing concepts freely, teaching the newcomers their adobe methods while adopting Spanish building technologies and modern innovations. Some Pueblos still live in large communal dwellings and reject electricity and piped water, as in Taos, but many others today live in houses that look depressingly suburban.

Herding livestock was an even easier adjustment. Cattle and sheep provided the same necessities as deer and buffalo and didn't have to be hunted. Besides, sheep supplied wool, which was simple to weave and much warmer than cotton.

The Pueblos quickly adopted Spanish weaving techniques and then passed them along to the Navajos, who had settled in the Southwest just a couple of centuries before the Spanish. A Navajo legend claims that Spider Man and Spider Woman taught them to weave, but the evidence is clear that their real benefactors were the Pueblos, whom they raided for a lot more than ideas and with whom they have maintained some enmity to the present day.

The Pueblos colored their wool with impermanent vegetable dyes, developed much earlier for their cotton cloth. The Navajos, however, experimented with durable and bright dyes introduced by the Spanish and soon surpassed their teachers in weaving skills. By the early nineteenth century the Spanish and Pueblos were acknowledging the proficiency of the Navajos and trading for their blankets. Some Pueblos continued to weave after that time, but they never made an effort to emulate the artistic and commercial success of their students.

The situation is somewhat similar in jewelry craftsmanship. The Pueblos mined turquoise in the Southwest, and made it into jewelry, before either the Spanish or the Navajos arrived in the region, and they continued to work primarily with turquoise and other stones even after the Spanish introduced metalsmithing. Some contemporary jewelers, particularly from Santo Domingo and Zuni, have achieved artistic and financial success with traditional materials and styles, but as with weaving, the Navajos on the whole were more adaptable and commercially successful.

Navajo artisans convinced the Spanish to teach them smithing about 1850, and began copying and modifying

Spanish silver work. They were making squash blossom necklaces and silver *concha* belts by the 1870s, using design ideas borrowed from Spanish silver bridles. In the next decade they discovered a technique for setting turquoise in silver, taking a precut stone and molding the metal to fit it.

Since these early days, for more than a century now, Navajo silver work has been in high demand with traders and collectors. One Pueblo group, the Hopi, began producing exceptional metal jewelry in recent decades, but most Pueblo artisans maintain their historic attachment to turquoise.

In pottery the Pueblos preserve tradition with similar dedication. They still make pots by hand, as their ancestors did, without the use of a potter's wheel. Coiling ropes of clay on top of one another to build up the walls of a piece, they then smooth the surface to eliminate any trace of the coils. The pots are fired outside in the open, instead of in a kiln, with dried dung cakes as the most common fuel.

Pottery has been the most refined Pueblo craft for hundreds of years, and it is the only one that the Navajos haven't borrowed. Skills began to decline around the turn of the century—after the railroad brought enamelware, tin pails and other manufactured kitchen products to the area—but a significant renaissance began in the 1920s and has continued since.

Much of the stimulation for the pottery renaissance came from the village of San Ildefonso, just north of Santa Fe. The most famous residents of the pueblo, Maria and Julian Martinez, developed a distinctive style of black pottery inspired by old fragments discovered in an archaeological dig. Maria was already an accomplished potter in 1919 when Julian worked out the technique for producing matte black designs on her polished black pots. The style was an immediate success, to such a degree that Maria began signing her work in 1925, something Pueblo artists had not done before.

The black-on-black style is still popular among San Ildefonso potters, but many of the best have branched out in different directions. Rose Gonzales introduced intaglio techniques in the 1930s, carving designs on the surface of the vessel. Later Blue Corn revived the polychromatic style that had been common in the village in the nineteenth century. Her work influenced Popovi Da, Maria and Julian's son, to do some similar pots, even while he was assisting his mother at her work and developing a new firing technique of his own to make two-tone pieces of black and sienna. Popovi's son, Tony Da, established his reputation by decorating work with inlaid turquoise and *heishi* (shell).

Some of these same styles and techniques are also found at Santa Clara, which is close to San Ildefonso both in distance and in the fame of its pottery. Several decades ago at the pueblo, Lela and Van Gutierrez developed a polychrome form, which their children, Margaret and Luther, further refined. Sarafina and Geronimo Tafoya established a dynasty of potters that produced work in a variety of modes, including the polished, carved ware that is most characteristic of Santa Clara. Their talented heirs include Margaret Tafoya, Camilio Tafoya, Christina Naranjo, Teresita Naranjo, Joseph Lonewolf and Grace Medicine Flower.

At Hopi, Nampeyo inspired a dramatic resurgence of pottery earlier this century. Fascinated by shards of ancient Hopi work, she created the distinctive orange ware that became the dominant form in her village. Her daughters, granddaughters, and great-granddaughters, who normally use the Nampeyo name with their own in signing work, perpetuated the tradition. In recent decades some Hopi artists ventured into other styles, such as the white clay forms of Joy Navasie (Frogwoman) and Helen Naha (Featherwoman).

At Acoma, Lucy Lewis and Marie Chino helped establish a distinctive white-clay pottery, shaped very thin and decorated with intricate geometric and animal designs or with more conventional polychrome patterns. Chino's daughters—Rose Garcia, Grace Chino and Carrie Charlie—and four of the Lewis children—Emma Mitchell, Delores Garcia, Mary Histia and Ann Hansen—refined the style. The polychrome work at Zia, a well-established tradition in the pueblo, resembles some of the Acoma pottery, but is made with red clay.

A few villages, most notably Cochiti, specialize in clay figurines instead of pots. In some ways these pieces reflect the curio orientation in Pueblo pottery that was popular before the current renaissance began, but many of them today are exquisite creations, particularly the storyteller figures of Helen Cordero and other talented Cochiti artisans.

The work of these and other potters is the most visible sign today of Pueblo endurance and devotion to cultural heritage. Styles and design patterns may be in flux, as they always have been to some degree, but the substance of the craft has remained essentially unchanged over the centuries. Pueblo artisans are still using basic elements of the original techniques the Anasazi developed about fifteen hundred years ago, and much of the inspiration for their current designs goes back to that earlier period.

Two of the most powerful nations of the modern world, imperial Spain and the United States, conquered the Pueblos during periods of vigorous expansion. They caused some changes in the way of life, but neither managed to complete the spiritual and cultural conquest they intended. Pueblo pottery, religion, social customs and other traditional practices remain a magnificent demonstration of the strength and vitality of a culture that developed long before either of the conquering nations.

Chapter Two
♦♦♦♦♦♦♦♦♦♦♦
Our Spanish Forefathers

O UR BRITISH forefathers came to the New World to escape from the old. They felt hopeless about their lives in England and wanted to carve a different destiny for themselves.

Our Spanish forefathers felt hopeless about nothing. They came to the New World to reshape it in the image of the old, on behalf of God, gold and glory. Santa Fe was one of several miscalculations along the way. *La Villa Real de la Santa Fe de San Francisco*, the Royal City of the Holy Faith of St. Francis, did become an Old World city, as the name implies, but it yielded little gold or glory and the native population took to God only in limited and frustrating ways.

Some of the first Spanish explorers to reach New Mexico might have guessed this fate in realistic moments, but hope blinded the *conquistadores*. Cabeza de Vaca, shipwrecked on the Texas coast in 1528, wandered the Southwest for eight years. Though his most impressive discovery was Indians living in permanent mud homes, growing corn, beans and squash, that was enough to inspire visions of cities of gold. A second small party, led by Friar Marcos de Niza, did not find the fabulous cities— but did report seeing them from a distant hilltop.

The Friar's account stimulated a major expedition, headed by Francisco Vásquez de Coronado, that included three hundred volunteer soldiers, a band of Christian missionaries and several hundred Mexican Indian servants. Coronado baptized some Indians in the Southwest between 1540 and 1542, but returned to Mexico City without glory or gold. His quest had cost about two million dollars in today's currency. Refusing to believe that the investment was futile, the authorities tried the explorer for not looking far enough.

The first colonizing expedition left Mexico City in 1598 with 130 families, hundreds of Indian servants and "eight seraphic, apostolic, preaching priests," as they were described. They entered New Mexico with a flagellation rite, a fiesta and a play. Arriving near the present-day site of El Paso on Holy Thursday, the colonists observed the day with medieval *penitente* ceremonies that are still practiced to some degree in northern New Mexico. A chronicler among the colonists wrote that "the soldiers, with cruel scourges, beat their backs unmercifully until the camp ran crimson with their blood. The humble Franciscan friars, barefoot and clothed in cruel thorny girdles, devoutly chanted their doleful hymns."

Shortly afterwards, the group encountered some friendly Indians and celebrated possession of the new land. After a fiesta the colonists presented an edifying drama to the Indians, showing the natives joyfully welcoming the first priests and begging for baptism. The play may have been entertaining, but it wasn't much as prophecy.

The colonists settled originally near the San Juan Pueblo, north of Santa Fe, and immediately began the search for riches and souls. Typically, their reports to

Mexico City were grander than their real discoveries. Within a few years the Franciscans claimed sixty thousand Indian converts, probably three times the total native population of the area. One of the pioneers who traveled the region speculated on the local geography, reckoning that New Mexico was a peninsula extending northward between Newfoundland and China, within sight of the latter at some point yet to be found. The reports ran so contrary to actual experience that the main chronicler of the colony was later tried for writing "beautiful but untrue accounts."

Decimated by starvation, desertion and Indian revolts, the San Juan settlement was abandoned in 1610 in favor of a new beginning at Santa Fe. Life remained fragile and rough for the colonists in the new location, but they gradually began to adjust their expectations and adapt to the environment. They survived a meager existence for several generations before famine and religious passion created a major disturbance.

In the l670s a drought forced both colonists and Indians into subsisting on hides boiled with roots and herbs, a diet probably related to the epidemic that followed. In the midst of this distress, the Spanish governor decided to obliterate all traces of Pueblo religion. Many of the natives had accepted Catholicism, but only as a supplement to their traditional beliefs, which they never considered dropping. The governor tried 47 Pueblo shamans for sorcery and hanged three. For his own good he should have executed at least four, because one of those released, Popé, was a charismatic and powerful leader.

Popé devised a masterful plan for a mass insurrection against the Spanish and organized the various pueblos to carry it out simultaneously. On August 10, 1680, the Indians began slaughtering the Spanish, starting with outlying villages and moving toward Santa Fe. Spanish survivors barricaded themselves in the Palace of the Governors as the Indians burned the town around them. Eventually the Pueblos, who have never enjoyed war, allowed the survivors to flee south to El Paso.

The Spanish colonists remained there for 12 years, until new recruits could be mustered for a reconquest. To lead the return, the Viceroy of New Spain chose Don Diego de Vargas, a proven soldier from an illustrious Madrid family. De Vargas's initial expedition to Santa Fe in 1692 encountered no resistance, and he went back to Mexico proclaiming a peaceful victory. When De Vargas returned the following year, however, to reestablish the colony, the Indians fought back. He had to take the Palace of the Governors by force, and afterwards he executed 70 of the defenders and enslaved four hundred others. The Pueblos continued to resist for three bloody years before the Spanish completed the reconquest.

The colonists had to rebuild Santa Fe totally. The Palace of the Governors was intact, and the walls of the San Miguel Mission were still standing, but the Indians had razed everything else. As before, the settlers built in adobe, supplementing their own knowledge of the material with concepts borrowed from the Pueblos. They made adobe bricks with mud and straw, drying them in the sun at the building site. They bonded the blocks together with wet adobe and later plastered them with the same mixture to make walls that were too thick to be pierced by arrows.

The Spanish kept their houses close to the ground, with low ceilings and flat roofs, never going over one story until the late nineteenth century. Pine logs, or *vigas*, laid on top of the walls, supported the earthen roof, composed of brush and soil. The home of an *hidalgo*, a gentleman, differed from that of a peasant primarily in the length of the vigas, which determined the size of the house. Everyone had floors of dirt mixed with animal blood to produce a hard clay surface. Most rooms contained a small corner fireplace designed to take upright logs.

The furnishings in homes were simple and crude during the colonial period. Even hidalgos owned little beyond hand-hewn chests, benches, stools and a table. The settlers made most of the furniture, since Santa Fe's isolation precluded the importation of many bulky goods.

The religious art that decorated homes and churches was easier to bring from Spain and Mexico, though much of it was crafted locally, too. *Retablos,* religious paintings on flat boards, were almost always imported until the nineteenth century because drawing skills and paints were rare in the early colony. More people knew woodcarving, which they used in decorating vigas and furniture and in making *bultos,* wooden statues. Most of the *bultos* were images of saints, called *santos,* though carvers also made *reredoses,* or altar screens, and *muertes,* the distinctive death carts that are a vivid symbol of the colonists' struggle with life.

Doctors were scarce in the colony. The only "surgeon and dentist" on record in the eighteenth century seems to have impressed residents more with his tools than his cures. He had "two cases for instruments, one with five razors, and whetstone, and the other one with six lancets trimmed with tortoise shell and silver." During most of the colonial period, residents relied on home remedies, using herbs, other plants and whiskey distilled in the area.

In the homes of *los ricos,* the rich, these medical staples were kept in locked storerooms, along with hanging meat cuts and strings of dried fruit and chile. Wealth was based on the amount of land and sheep owned, but everyone was a farmer. In the summer the colonists enjoyed fresh corn, chiles, beans, onions and various fruits, but for most of the year they ate dried produce and cornmeal made into tortillas. The women cooked meals in the fireplace in heavy kettles or outside in *hornos,* beehive-shaped adobe ovens, and served the food on pottery, much of it made by the Pueblos.

While working at home, women wore full, short skirts of serge and tight, low-necked blouses that some early American visitors considered indecent. When they left the house, ladies who could afford it wrapped themselves in imported shawls, or, for special occasions, dressed in European finery. They often used red clay for rouge, but switched to a heavy white powder of ground bones for *fandangos*, or dances.

Men often had a more extensive and expensive wardrobe than women, because of their exclusive hold on official and ceremonial roles in the colony. Hidalgos needed fancy uniforms, with gold lace if possible, for military formalities. At other times they wore woolen pantaloons, leather jackets and high boots, well suited for riding. Wool *serapes* and imported flat *sombreros* protected them from the weather.

The residents wove the fabrics for most of their clothes. The usual cloth was *sabanilla*, a woolen plain-weave they made in large quantities for basic garments and bedding. It was sometimes embroidered with floral or geometric designs in the distinctive long *colcha* stitch.

In the latter colonial period weaving became a refined craft in New Mexico. At the same time the Navajos were developing their weaving skills, the Spanish independently established a similar tradition, known as the Rio Grande style. Design patterns from the Orient—transmitted through fabrics made in Saltillo, Mexico—heavily influenced both groups. Rio Grande blankets and rugs are not as well-known today as their Navajo counterparts, but Spanish artisans did some exceptional work.

Life was austere in the colony on the whole, crafted as it was by hand from scarce resources, but it did not lack gaiety. Fiestas in celebration of Mardi Gras, Easter, Christmas, saints' days, marriages and other special occasions were frequent and important. When Mexico won its independence from Spain in 1821, the festivities in

Santa Fe lasted five days. On the first morning the residents raised the new flag and then joined in a spontaneous parade. Afterwards everyone gathered at the Palace. The head of the city council led a cotillion, which opened a grand *baile*, or ball, where celebrants danced to lively guitar and violin versions of the same tunes that were played more solemnly in church. A puritanical American trader who happened to be in town was shocked at the revelry: "All classes abandoned themselves to the most reckless dissipation," including "vice and licentiousness of every description," which went on "night and day" with "no time for sleep."

A generation later, when the U.S. Army seized Santa Fe from Mexico, there were no celebrations. Suddenly New Mexico was severed from its historical and cultural roots in the Spanish colonial empire. The residents gradually adjusted to the new situation, after a few ineffective attempts at insurrection, but for many years afterwards there were more Army band concerts than fiestas on the plaza.

Fortunately, the Spanish heritage was too strong to perish, despite the attempts of some early Americans to destroy it. Much of the native population still knows and uses the Spanish language, though they have also mastered English and can now avoid the property swindles perpetrated on their grandparents. The U.S. Army suppressed the annual fiesta in honor of Don Diego de Vargas and his feats of the 1690s, but the fiesta was revived later and De Vargas is once again celebrated as a legendary hero, better known locally than George Washington. Spanish Catholic traditions, so different from those of the conquering soldiers, have persisted, from delightful Christmas customs to *penitente* flagellations at Easter.

The strength of the Spanish heritage today is particularly evident in the vitality of colonial crafts. Weaving and woodcarving died out in Santa Fe in the late nineteenth century, but the local traditions were maintained and refined in small mountain villages north of the city. The recent work of weavers Teresa Archuleta Sagel, Juanita Jaramillo, Maria Vergara-Wilson, and the Trujillo, Ortega and Cordova families reflects a commitment to preserve the Rio Grande style.

Vergara-Wilson, among others, has helped to resurrect *colcha* stitchery, while Eliseo and Paula Rodriquez have inspired new respect for the old art of straw appliqué on wood. Leo Salazar, Horacio Valdez, Anita Romero Jones, Felix López, Eluid Martinez, Ben Ortega and several members of the López family in Cordova have all carved *santos* as reverent and expressive as any made locally in past centuries.

Felipe Archuleta took the woodworking tradition in a new direction, creating whimsical sculptures of various animals. Other carvers, including Alonzo Jimenez, Jimbo Davila, Max Alvarez, and Felipe's son Leroy Archuleta, continue today in the same vein. The coyotes these artisans crafted became so popular that poor, mass-produced imitations are now cluttering the shelves of almost every shop in Santa Fe.

As long as its cultural heritage is an inspiration, Santa Fe will stay heavily Spanish. The colonists didn't find, or fully convert, many Indians, but they did entrench their way of life in an area very remote from home. Four centuries later, Santa Fe remains an outpost of the Old World in the New.

Chapter Three

◆◆◆◆◆◆◆◆◆◆◆

The Army and the Art Colony

IN SANTA FE the term *Anglo* has very broad applica-
tion. Used for almost anyone who is not Hispanic or
Indian, it is a polite way of saying non-native, or outsider,
in contrast with the more pejorative *gringo*. Residents
have conferred the title, at times at least, on Italians, Jews,
African Americans and even an occasional Briton.

The first Anglos to visit Santa Fe were escorted into
town under military guard, as prisoners, just a few years
before the city's 200th anniversary. A small party of U.S.
explorers trespassed on the Spanish empire accidentally
in the winter of 1805–1806. Under orders from President
Thomas Jefferson to find the sources of western tributar-
ies of the Mississippi River, Lieutenant Zebulon Pike and
his men stumbled instead upon the headwaters of the Rio
Grande in the Colorado Rockies. A Spanish militia unit
arrested the Americans and took them to Santa Fe for
questioning, treating them more as curiosities than as
captives.

Local policy toward Anglo visitors changed considerably in the following two decades. When Mexico won its

independence from Spain, the new republic wanted to establish good relations with its republican neighbors to the northeast. In 1821 a Mexican militia unit from Santa Fe encountered a group of Missourians, wandering the plains trading with Indians. The Santa Feans invited the traders to return home with them to sell their wares, opening the Santa Fe Trail.

Thousands of Anglos came and went over the trail between Missouri and Santa Fe in the next half century. At its peak of activity trade along the route employed ten thousand men and grossed millions of dollars annually for both Mexican and American merchants.

The existence of the trail made Santa Fe a natural target for the United States in the 1846–1848 war with Mexico. President James K. Polk started the war mainly to acquire California from Mexico, to realize America's "manifest destiny" of expanding to the Pacific Ocean. Santa Fe was occupied on the way to California.

The U.S. Army stayed for the rest of the nineteenth century and became an important presence in the city. The soldiers' impressions were not particularly favorable. One of them wrote home about his "perfect contempt" for the city and another called it "the Siberia of America." To them, Santa Fe was, as a third soldier described it, "a dirty, filthy place built entirely of mud." The Army erected a sawmill as soon as it arrived, with the intention of replacing adobe buildings with "proper" wood structures.

This feeling about adobe prevailed among Anglo residents until the early twentieth century. There was still a good deal of adobe construction in Santa Fe in the territorial period, before New Mexico gained statehood in 1912, but almost everyone who could afford it wanted to use milled lumber and brick for trim at least. Residents modified many of the city's historic homes in the territorial style, perhaps adding decorative layers of brick along roof lines and Greek Revival doors, windows and portals. The ideal for most Anglo residents was an all-brick house with a pitched roof, like those in their Eastern home towns.

Attitudes changed along with Anglo settlement patterns about the time that statehood was granted. With New Mexico firmly incorporated into the United States, and the Navajos and Apaches of the area conquered, the U.S. Army moved out. As the soldiers left, anthropologists and artists moved in.

The anthropologists were attracted initially by the work of Adolph Bandelier, a Swiss scholar of international reputation who lived in Santa Fe in the 1880s. Bandelier's studies of the Pueblos stimulated considerable interest in North American prehistory. In 1907 the Archaeological Institute of America opened a center in Santa Fe, the School of American Research. The early leaders of the school, particularly Edgar Hewett and Sylvanus Morley, replaced the Army colonels as the prime molders of Anglo opinion in the city.

Unlike their predecessors, the anthropologists understood and appreciated the historical character of Santa Fe and wanted it preserved. They helped to inspire a revival of the Spanish Pueblo architectural style that still influences much new construction in the city.

Painters and writers of the early Santa Fe art colony assisted energetically in the preservation efforts. They began arriving in town about a decade after the anthropologists and soon had the scholars outnumbered. By the 1920s the art colony was a major force in Santa Fe life; since then it has been the primary Anglo influence in the city.

The first Anglo artists in the area arrived in Taos in the late 1890s. Ernest Blumenschein was a popular and successful artist in the East when he passed through the village doing illustrations for a magazine article. He and his friend Bert Phillips, another established artist, were attracted immediately to the serenity and primitive charm of New Mexico, and they soon moved permanently to Taos.

Blumenschein and Phillips, along with several other recognized artists who followed them west, formed the Taos Society of Artists in 1912. Mostly educated in Paris, the society members were highly skilled within the representational traditions of their day. Their literal documentation of New Mexican life was so popular elsewhere that the Atchison, Topeka, and Santa Fe Railroad commissioned them to do paintings to hang in its offices and print on calendars, as advertising in the early days of the tourism business.

The Santa Fe art colony began forming in the early 1910s. The leading figures of the first decade were Robert Henri and John Sloan, both of whom continued to live mainly in New York, though Sloan maintained a summer home in Santa Fe for more than 30 years.

A number of less established artists moved to the city permanently in the same period. Five of these, all under 30 years of age and newly arrived in town, banded together for a show at the Museum of Fine Arts in 1921, calling themselves *Los Cinco Pintores*, "the Five Painters." A spirited group, influenced by Cézanne and Post-Impressionism, they reacted against the prestige of the Taos Society and declared that their purpose was "to take art to the people and not surrender to commercialism." The work of Jozef Bakos, Fremont Ellis, Walter Mruk, Willard Nash and Will Shuster seems fairly traditional today, but that was not the way the artists intended it or the public originally received it.

In the 1920s the international avant-garde invaded New Mexico. Mable Dodge Luhan, once described as "a reposeful hurricane," moved her radical salon from New York City to Taos during the conservative backlash following World War I. She "willed," as she put it, a global roster of visitors, including D. H. Lawrence, Max Weber,

Paul and Rebecca Strand (who brought Georgia O'Keeffe with them), John Marin, Marsden Hartley and Andrew Dasburg. Edmund Wilson described the resident circle in 1930 as an "extraordinary population of rich people, writers, and artists who pose as Indians, cowboys, prospectors, desperadoes, Mexicans and other nearly extinct species." Two of Luhan's guests—O'Keeffe and Dasburg—stayed in the area and became legendary presences.

During the Depression and into the 1950s the art colony of Santa Fe grew as slowly as the rest of the city. A few major artists, including Laura Gilpin, Eliot Porter and Agnes Martin, moved to the area in this period, but the next large influx of Anglo artists did not occur until the 1960s, when Paul Sarkisian and Fritz Scholder started an immigration that later included Larry Bell, Ken Price, Bruce Nauman, Bob Wade, Rick Dillingham, Glenda Goodacre, Judy Chicago, Herb Ritts and Terry Allen. In 1970 Clinton Adams moved the Tamarind Institute from Los Angeles to Albuquerque, stimulating a significant upsurge in printmaking in New Mexico and establishing Albuquerque as another center for artists in the state.

Most of the new arrivals in the last couple of decades have been young artists who have come to the area without established reputations. Many of them have made distinctive use of the local environment, both cultural and natural, in their work. Luis Jimenez developed sophisticated fiberglass sculptures of cowboy-and-Indian scenes that reflected the popular mythology of the West in glittery plastic. Ken Saville's drawings and constructions placed human frailty and darkness in the vibrant context of colorful Southwestern images. The New Mexico landscape and light still inspire many painters, both abstract and representational, as they have for a century now.

Photography has thrived as an art form in Santa Fe for many years. Most major American photographers have worked in the area and many moved here, including Eliot

Porter, Beaumont Newhall, Paul Caponigro, Meridel Rubenstein, and Douglas Kent Hall. Fine crafts are also an established specialization in town, and in recent years printmaking has gained in popularity with support from the facilities at Hand Graphics and Graphics Workshop.

The College of Santa Fe's Sculpture Project encourages large-scale three-dimensional work, but the center of production and exhibition is the Shidoni Foundry and Gallery in Tesuque, five acres of fun. The work ranges from Western bronzes to towering abstract pieces.

While Anglo artists continue to play a pivotal role in the Santa Fe scene, the art colony today is much more multiethnic than in the past. A number of Indian painters, printmakers and sculptors—including Jaune Quick-to-See Smith, Emmi Whitehorse, Allan Houser and Bob Haozous—have attracted national attention using Native American references and elements of style in work that is contemporary in concept and resonance. Many local Hispanic artists, such as Luis Tapia and Frederico Vigil, move beyond traditional formats but maintain a strong sensitivity for cultural roots.

The diversity of people, media and styles makes the art colony today less cohesive than in the past and less focused in its local influence, but its impact on Santa Fe is more pervasive than ever. The adobe-hating soldiers of the U.S. Army might have found another way to California if they had known the future they were opening in Santa Fe. Certainly Ernest Blumenschein would be startled by what he began. He would understand, no doubt, why the art colony has continued to flourish, but would be amused, at best, to learn that it is as full of galleries and collectors as the fast-paced art centers of the East that he left so far behind in the 1890s.

PART TWO

THE
LIVING
MUSEUM

Chapter Four

♦♦♦♦♦♦♦♦♦♦♦

Exploring
the Plaza and Downtown

TEN YEARS before the Pilgrims landed at Plymouth Rock, some fifty Spanish soldiers and their families erected crude mud and timber shelters around the central plaza of Santa Fe. From that bare beginning—for almost four centuries—the plaza has been the center of Santa Fe life and the first destination for most visitors.

The original plaza was larger than it is today, extending east in a rectangular shape to the site of the present cathedral. In the seventeenth century, while the Puritans settled the rest of New England, mounted soldiers in medieval armor used the area as an assembly and drill ground. Anything of a public nature—proclamations, games, markets, fiestas, even bullfights—occurred there as well. The plaza was where residents celebrated Mexican independence from Spain in 1821 and where General Kearney proclaimed the annexation of New Mexico by the United States to an unenthusiastic citizenry in 1846. Today it is the site of Indian Market, Spanish Market and much of Fiesta—annual occasions when the plaza still tolerates hordes of happy traders and rowdy celebrants. Even an

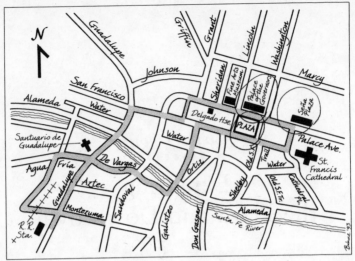

A Downtown Walking Tour around the Plaza
and down Guadalupe Street

average tourist day now, particularly in the summer, can give the area the aura of a carnival.

The plaza's most tumultuous period, however, was in the mid-nineteenth century, when it served as the western terminus of the Santa Fe Trail. As the Yankee traders approached Santa Fe at the end of their arduous journey from Missouri, they charged the town center, shouting and cracking 12-foot whips, scattering dust, dogs and chickens in all directions. Before slowing down, the long wagon trains, carrying about five thousand pounds of merchandise each, raced in a great spiral about the four sides of the plaza. Crowds gathered quickly, eager for outside news, new provisions and the chance to make some money from the high-living, road-weary visitors. As the plaza filled with wagons, the traders made their way around the gambling rooms that lined nearby streets, playing monte and dancing fandangos with the "relentlessly coquettish *mujeres* of Santa Fe," as one trader described the ladies.

Facing north from the plaza, toward the Palace of the Governors, try to imagine another raucous moment from the past. In 1680 about twenty-five hundred Pueblo Indians looked angrily in the same direction, chanting songs of vengeance day and night, determined to drive the Spanish from the Pueblo land. Barricaded in the Palace, which was larger then, were a thousand terrified people and many more starving sheep, mules, horses, goats and cattle.

The Indians had already killed several hundred Spaniards in villages north of Santa Fe and they were now plundering and burning the church at the east end of the plaza. One of the Pueblo leaders, wrapped in red taffeta taken from the church, offered the Spanish a choice of two crosses—red for war or white for a peaceful departure. The Spanish elected to stay and fight, but they didn't have a chance. The water supply for the Palace crossed by the plaza in an irrigation ditch; the Indians easily diverted the *acequia* and kept the Spanish out for more than 12 years. The peaceful Pueblos forced the Spanish empire into a more serious retreat than the mighty Aztec and Incan warriors ever managed.

The Spanish recaptured the Palace and the plaza in 1693, but this feat may not be very evident in the area today. The Pueblos have come back in force in recent years, bearing pots and bracelets this time instead of torches. Only Indian artisans are allowed to sell work under the portal of the Palace, and they are there almost every day, stoically accepting the stares and questions of curious visitors along with their money.

Some of the best Indian art galleries in town are also on the plaza and along adjacent streets. Packard's, Dewey Galleries and the museum shop in the Palace, all directly on the plaza, provide a good introduction to the range and quality of contemporary Indian work. Other nearby Indian galleries are noted in Chapter 15.

The Palace of the Governors

In continuous use since 1610, the Palace is the oldest government building in the United States. Over a hundred rulers—Spanish, Pueblo, Mexican and American—have occupied the building. From this spot some of them claimed sovereignty over half of the present-day United States, east to the Mississippi River, west to the Pacific Ocean and south into the Mexican state of Chihuahua.

The original structure, built by the first Spanish governor, Pedro de Peralta, extended much farther north and west than the present-day Palace. The enclosed central patio was large enough for a 10-acre vegetable garden. There was no portal then, but there were defense towers on the two corners facing the plaza.

When the Indians evicted the Spanish in 1680, they transformed the Palace into a typical Pueblo village. The small Spanish windows and doors were blocked up, and rooms were entered from the top by ladders. Like the Taos Pueblo, the structure grew upwards, probably to three or four stories. One of the towers was converted into a kiva, which the returning Spanish reluctantly used for their own worship for over a decade, until they completed a new parish church.

Almost everything except the roof beams, or vigas, was originally made of dirt. The walls, then as now, were adobe. The dirt floor was mixed with animal blood to pack it and produce a sheen. It wasn't until the late nineteenth century that tin replaced the dirt roof that was piled several feet high above the vigas. Before then at least one resident of Santa Fe called it the "roof garden": "Most every desert plant grew and flowered and died a natural death in the five feet of earth which held the moisture of ordinary downpours but let the cloudbursts trickle through. The inside was really the only place where we had any need for umbrellas; outside the continuous line of portals protected us." The place has seldom, if ever, looked like a palace.

Probably the best-known today of the Palace's many residents was U.S. Territorial Governor Lew Wallace, author of *Ben Hur*, who lived there in the 1880s. Wallace's description of his writing chamber would probably have applied to many rooms in the Palace at the time: "The walls were grimy, the undressed boards of the floor rested flat upon the ground; the cedar rafters, rain-stained as those in the dining-hall of Cedric the Saxon, and overweighted by tons and tons of mud composing the roof, had the threatening downward curvature of a shipmate's cutlass."

The construction and size of the building have always made it relatively expensive to maintain. Spanish, Mexican and U.S. governors were constantly petitioning their various central governments for money for repairs, never getting as much as they requested. At the turn of the century, the upkeep costs made the Palace a political football. The U.S. government granted the building, along with its maintenance costs, to the territorial government of New Mexico. The governor protested, saying the territory couldn't afford it. He offered it to the Smithsonian Institution, which rejected it as an unmanageable property. Stuck with possession, the legislature decided in 1909 to transform the Palace into the Museum of New Mexico and appropriated funds for its restoration.

At first the Palace housed all of the museum. Since then separate facilities have been built in Santa Fe for the state's collection of fine art, folk art, Indian art and anthropology. See Chapter 7 for more information on the various facilities.

The Museum of Fine Arts

The Museum of Fine Arts, situated directly west of the Palace, had an unusual beginning among American art museums. Most museums originate as repositories for lifelong collections of art patrons. When the Museum of Fine Arts opened in 1917, it was the first in the United States—and it has been one of the few since then—inspired by local artists for exhibits of their current work.

As soon as the legislature established the Museum of New Mexico in the Palace of the Governors, the first director, Dr. Edgar Hewett, began thinking about a separate museum for art. At first he set up a small gallery within the Palace and provided free studios to artists in the back of the building. Predictably, demands on the space grew, and within a few years Hewett managed to convince the legislature to build an art museum across the street from the Palace.

Robert Henri and John Sloan, established artists from the East who spent considerable time in Santa Fe, advised Hewett on policy for the new museum. They advocated the "open-door" approach that the museum took for many years, which allowed any local artist to exhibit new work on a first-come, first-served basis. No effort was made to acquire a collection of Old Masters from past centuries and distant places, though gradually the museum did begin building a collection of New Mexican artists' works.

After a few decades the local collection was substantial, featuring some important works by the earliest artists in the area, who were becoming known by then as Old Masters themselves. As the collection became more valuable, art patrons of the city became active in the affairs of the museum, and the artists lost their ease of access. The quality of exhibitions has been more consistent since the elimination of the open-door policy, but some of the museum's vitality may have been lost in the process.

The museum was built on land once occupied by the western part of the Palace of the Governors and later, in the nineteenth century, by U.S. Army barracks. Completed in 1917, the new structure was an early and influential expression of the modern Spanish Pueblo architectural style. Its massive walls, terraces and recessions reflect the organic lines of Pueblo buildings. The Spanish Franciscan mission churches, particularly the one at Acoma, inspired the St. Francis Auditorium, an entrancing spot for the concerts and other performances held here. On the museum's completion residents and visitors alike hailed the synthesis of traditions represented in the new building, and it became a model for the style that still guides much architectural design in the city.

See Chapter 7 for information on the museum's exhibits and schedule.

West Palace Avenue

In the nineteenth century, farther west of the plaza along Palace Avenue and the side-streets, you would have found Santa Fe's rowdy gambling district. Buffalo hunters, *vaqueros*, politicians, traders and soldiers came here to drink the raw whiskey called Taos Lightning and to find love, or a semblance of it, with lavender-powdered *señoritas* in black veils.

The strongest personality of them all was the beautiful and shrewd Doña Tules Barcelo, who owned the largest and fanciest of the gambling halls and a bank as well. One puritanical trader, who referred to the *cantinas* as "pandemoniums," called Doña Tules a woman "of very loose habits" and was shocked that she was "openly received in the first circles of society." He imagined with pleasure how she would have been socially rejected in Eastern cities, but felt exasperated that she wouldn't have cared. Ruth Laughlin has told Doña Tules's story in fictional form in *The Wind Leaves No Shadows* (Caxton Printers, 1978).

Palace Avenue, though much tamer today, is still worth

a short visit. Just west of the Museum of Fine Arts and across the street is the Delgado House, now used as a bank office. Originally the residence of Felipe Delgado, a major trader on the Santa Fe Trail, the adobe house was finished elaborately for its day with a wooden balcony, window casings and decorative trim. It was restored in the 1970s by John Gaw Meem, the local architect whose integrity and persistence contributed enormously to the development and maintenance of Spanish Pueblo design standards in the city.

After another block Palace Avenue jogs south to intersect with San Francisco Street. From this point our walking tour makes a one-mile loop to Guadalupe Street and back, though weary or hurried walkers can return to the plaza via San Francisco. For those doing it all, the next point of interest is the Santuario de Guadalupe, one block west on San Francisco and a couple of blocks south on Guadalupe.

Santuario de Nuestra Señora de Guadalupe

Built in the last few years of the eighteenth century, the Chapel of Our Lady of Guadalupe was designed and constructed in the style typical of New Mexican church architecture of that period. The walls, floor and roof were adobe, and the shape was cruciform. The three-tiered tower contained sand-cast copper bells.

When a new, larger church was built on the property in 1961, the chapel was no longer used for mass. After several years of neglect, the parishioners restored it in its original style. The attention to detail in the preservation effort is seen in the red altar wall, where ox blood was added to the plaster to reproduce the eighteenth-century appearance.

The Santuario is open to visitors Monday through Saturday, 9:00 to 12:00 and 1:00 to 4:00, throughout the year. Admission is free, but donations are appreciated. Give generously—many repairs are needed.

Guadalupe Street

A few blocks south of the Santuario on Guadalupe Street is the Atchison, Topeka, and Santa Fe Railroad depot. Between these two landmarks is a rapidly developing complex of shops and restaurants along with a couple of historical curiosities.

At the corner of Guadalupe and Garfield, across from the depot, is the University Plaza, now used for offices and shops but originally built as a school in the 1880s by Protestant evangelists hoping to convert "heathen" New Mexicans. The missionaries intended their "University of New Mexico" to be a fountainhead of "moral education" in the recently conquered Catholic territory, but they found life in Santa Fe so disagreeable and the residents so unheeding that they soon abandoned the project.

The other historical curiosity of the area is the railroad itself. Despite its name, and the fact that it paralleled and replaced the Santa Fe Trail, the Atchison, Topeka, and Santa Fe Railroad never made it to Santa Fe. The city was one of the few in America unwilling to pay for rail service. Bishop Jean Baptiste Lamy argued passionately for the value of the railroad, but other civic leaders weren't interested in better connections to the rest of the country. All the bishop could obtain was a spur from the main line at a junction south of the city that is still named Lamy. The main line went to Albuquerque instead, stimulating its growth from a provincial village into New Mexico's most populous city.

Until recently the Guadalupe area remained an appendage of the railroad depot, occupied largely by freight warehouses. A slow but sustained renovation began in the 1970s, first on Guadalupe Street itself and later on the

side-streets. Now some people are calling the neighborhood Santa Fe's Soho. It's less fashionable and crowded
than the plaza or Canyon Road, but it does have a funky
spirit and more local shoppers.

For a real taste of the area, go west from Guadalupe on
Montezuma Avenue to the Sanbusco Center, a renovated
railyard warehouse now housing shops, galleries and restaurants. On Tuesday and Saturday from early summer
through October the Sanbusco parking lot comes alive
with the sounds and smells of the Farmer's Market. Farm-
ers and gardeners from all over northern New Mexico
sell vegetables, fruits, flowers, baked goods, fresh salsas,
pestos and other treats. The stalls are open from 7:00 to
noon, but the local color and selection begin to fade as
early as 8:00 or 9:00.

To return to San Francisco Street and the plaza, go
back to the Santuario, turn right on East De Vargas and
then left on Galisteo, a good street for browsing.

San Francisco Street

Named for St. Francis, the patron saint of Santa Fe, San
Francisco Street was established in its current course by
the mid-eighteenth century. The earliest extant map of
the city, done in the 1760s, shows the intersection of San
Francisco and Galisteo. "Camino de Galisteo" on the
map cuts through fields from the south and has very few
buildings on it. To the right at the intersection are adobe
buildings, mainly long and narrow, lining San Francisco
Street down to the parish church where the cathedral now
stands. To the left is a small residence, more fields and
then the large hacienda of Nicolás Ortiz III.

San Francisco Street today is a boutique row, particularly on the stretch from Galisteo to the plaza. Several
buildings that used to house offices and large stores have

been divided into mini-malls, with a variety of small, specialized shops. A few places offer distinctive merchandise, but most sell the same sort of schlock you find in any major tourist destination. Continue east on San Francisco one block beyond the plaza to St. Francis Cathedral.

Cathedral of St. Francis   *in Death Comes for the Archbishop*

The cathedral is the most visible legacy of the most influential person in local history, Bishop Jean Baptiste Lamy, whose bronze statue stands in front of the building. It's ironic that a Frenchman played such a major role in shaping the fortunes of a Spanish colonial town in the American West, and the irony shows in the Romanesque style of the cathedral, so different from the rest of the local architecture.

Willa Cather gracefully described Lamy's life in Santa Fe (as Bishop Latour) in *Death Comes for the Archbishop* (paperback edition, Vintage Books, 1990). Arriving in 1851 during a wild frontier period in the village, when the church's authority was disintegrating throughout the Southwest, Lamy energetically restored clerical influence, established schools and a hospital, and gradually instilled a sense of refinement into Santa Fe life. His own notion of refinement, unfortunately, always remained European, not fully sympathetic to local ways. His tastes, and his predilection for modern progress, had some adverse effects on the town, but he served with dedication and is remembered with respect.

Bishop Lamy wanted a cathedral in Santa Fe that expressed God's glory with the same magnificence as the churches in his native Auvergne. The parish church, or *parroquia,* which he used as his cathedral for many years, was a simple adobe structure started in 1714. Lamy and his French architects built the new cathedral around the old *parroquia*, making it much wider and half again as long but retaining and using the old church until the new one was completed.

The cornerstone, elaborately engraved for the occasion, was laid with high ceremony in 1869 and promptly stolen. Construction proceeded anyway, using stone from nearby quarries and Italian stone-cutters, and continued until 1886, the year after the bishop's retirement. The original French plans, which were never carried out fully, called for steeples rising 160 feet from the two towers.

The most interesting part of St. Francis Cathedral is what is left of the old *parroquia*, the Chapel of Our Lady of the Rosary. The choir loft and part of the walls were removed in constructing the new church, making the chapel smaller than before, but it has been in continuous use since 1718.

The chapel is dedicated to the oldest madonna in North America, a small sixteenth-century wooden statue carved in Mexico and brought to Santa Fe about 1625. She was originally known as Our Lady of the Assumption, but was renamed La Conquistadora (Our Lady of the Conquest) after she accompanied the Spanish in exile from 1680 to 1693 and returned with them as a protector during the reconquest from the Pueblos. The chapel was built in her honor on the site of the original parish church, which was destroyed by the Indians in 1680, and she has remained ever since the community's most important symbol of Spanish unity and religious devotion. After years of pressure from the Pueblos, the current archbishop gave La Conquistadora an additional name, *Nuestra Señora de la Paz* (Our Lady of Peace), to emphasize the ultimate result of the reconquest.

The cathedral is open to visitors daily from 6:00 to 6:00. There is no admission charge, but contributions are welcome. The adjacent Cathedral Park is a shady spot for resting or picnicking.

Seña Plaza ✗

Another of the heroes of the Spanish reconquest was Captain Arias de Quiros. His feats lag a reverential distance behind La Conquistadora's in Santa Fe history, but in his day he received the more tangible reward of a large land grant directly north of the cathedral site.

The captain's domain included all of the area now covered by the long, low portal that runs down Palace Avenue to Washington Street, and considerably more. Arias de Quiros cultivated most of the land and lived in a two-room house, nothing of which remains.

The courtyard of <u>Seña Plaza,</u> which can be entered directly across from the street in front of the cathedral, is one of the m<u>ost charming spots in downtown Santa</u> Fe. ✗ Lined with shops today, it was the scene of grand Spanish hospitality in the nineteenth century, hosted by Doña Isabel and Don José Seña. From a small house he inherited on the property, Don José gradually built a hacienda of 33 rooms. He and Doña Isabel and their 11 children occupied the south, east and west sides of the courtyard; horses, chickens and servants were quartered along the north front. The home was one story except on the west side, where outside stairways led up to a large ballroom, a chamber sufficient in size to hold the legislative assembly temporarily when the capitol burned in 1892. The second stories on the eastern and northern portions of the building were added in the 1920s during a dedicated and expert restoration.

There are two smaller courtyards along this block of Palace, on the way back to the central plaza. L. Bradford Prince owned the hacienda that now houses <u>The Shed</u> ✗

Restaurant, and his courtyard is a waiting area for patrons. Trujillo Plaza, at 109 East Palace, contains shops
today but has an infamous past. During World War II it
was an office for the Manhattan Project, which developed
the first atomic bomb in nearby Los Alamos. Even the
existence of Los Alamos was a carefully guarded secret,
so the scientists involved reported for duty and received
their mail at Trujillo Plaza.

Chapter Five
◆◆◆◆◆◆◆◆◆◆

Strolling Along the River

MOST great cities in the world sit alongside great rivers or oceans. The Spanish colonists placed Santa Fe on a river, but no one had illusions of grandeur about the little mountain creek. The Santa Fe River is as slow, irregular and inexpedient as the town it crosses.

In spite of this, the creek had a symbolic hold on the residents for many years. For one thing, it determined the pattern of the city's settlement. In the first two centuries new residents built streets and homes parallel to the river's course, seldom more than a few blocks from the water. In the early nineteenth century, when the Santa Fe Trail was opened, the city was described as "three streets wide and a mile long," following the path of the river.

The river also served in the first century of the city as the dividing line between social classes. The Spanish soldiers and priests lived north of the river, on the plaza side, and their Indian servants from Mexico lived on the south side. The Indians named their area *Analco*, meaning "the other side of the water."

The most important structure in the Barrio de Analco

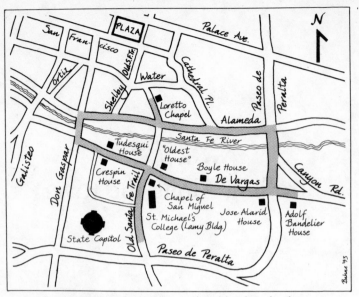

A Walk through Historic Neighborhoods along
the Santa Fe River

is the Chapel of San Miguel, built about 1610 to serve as the mission church for the Indian servants. The Pueblos gutted the church and razed all of the nearby homes during the 1680 Revolt. The residents who escaped the attack found safety in the Palace of the Governors and retreated to El Paso with the Spanish. Very few returned in the reconquest.

Santa Feans rebuilt the Barrio in the early eighteenth century. It was no longer strictly a district for servants, but class associations lingered for more than a hundred years. Some of the lovely homes in the neighborhood today originally belonged to laborers and low-ranking soldiers.

The best place to enter the Barrio de Analco is the corner of Don Gaspar and East De Vargas, which can be reached by following the river west along Alameda Street from the bridge on Old Santa Fe Trail and going south on Don Gaspar a short block. The original settlers laid out East De Vargas in 1610 and it still follows the same path as it did then.

Roque Tudesqui House (129–135 East De Vargas)

Roque Tudesqui was a successful trader in the early days of the Santa Fe Trail. Italian by birth—a rare nationality in Santa Fe at the time—he bought this house in 1841, when he was 40, shortly before his marriage to a local señorita.

There is no record of when the house was built, though a home was on or near the site in the mid-eighteenth century. The house is now divided into two private residences.

Gregorio Crespin House (132 East De Vargas)

General De Vargas granted this land to Juan de Leon Brito in the late seventeenth century as a reward for service in the Spanish reconquest of Santa Fe. The house was built early in the following century, between 1720 and 1750, according to tree-ring specimens taken from the vigas. A deed from 1747 shows the property being sold by Gregorio Crespin for 50 *pesos*.

The house grew larger over the years and certainly more valuable. In the mid-nineteenth century it contained five rooms, all opening onto the portal by the garden. Several decades later, the owner at the time added the territorial trim. The house remains a private residence today.

Chapel of San Miguel

The walls of the original chapel, dating to the earliest years of the Spanish settlement, are still intact, though they are not now visible. The Pueblos destroyed most of the church in the 1680 Revolt. When the Spanish rebuilt the chapel in 1710, they altered the shape of the structure and put up new outer walls alongside the old ones.

Worrying more about Indian raids in 1710 than they had in 1610, the Spanish restored the chapel as a fortress. Besides thickening the walls, they placed the windows high on the building and added adobe battlements to the roof. The roof line was changed again in the next century with the addition of a triple-tiered tower, which subsequently was displaced by the current square tower in the 1870s.

Used originally as the mission church for the Mexican Indian servants in the Barrio de Analco, the rebuilt chapel served the Spanish military in the eighteenth century. The Christian Brothers acquired the church in the mid-nineteenth century for the adjacent school, which they operated until recently. The Brothers still staff and maintain the chapel.

The most prominent feature of the interior is the fine *reredos*, or altar screen. Made in 1798, it was designed to display the small gilded statue of St. Michael, the patron of the chapel, and the six attached paintings. The statue, probably created in Mexico in the seventeenth century, was taken in procession throughout the frontier colony in 1709 to raise money, goods and services for the chapel's restoration.

Most of the paintings on the altar screen were done in Mexico in the eighteenth century. From left to right and top to bottom, the paintings depict St. Theresa of Avila, St. Michael, St. Gertrude, St. Francis of Assisi, Jesus and St. Louis. Early Franciscan missionaries did the paintings hanging midway down the nave to illustrate the Bible to the Indians. The one showing Christ on the cross is on buffalo hide, and the other, of Christ the Good Shepherd, is on deerskin.

The worn bell displayed in the gift shop, which once hung in the tower, was made in 1856. Defects in the sand-casting make the date appear to be 1356, but it is not that old.

The chapel is open to visitors daily from 9:00 to 4:30, except Sunday, when it opens at 1:00. Mass on Sunday is at 5:00. Donations are appreciated; there is no admission charge.

St. Michael's College

Just south of the chapel on Old Santa Fe Trail is the building the Christian Brothers used for many years as St. Michael's College. The Brothers sold the property in 1965 to the state of New Mexico, which named it the Lamy Building and filled it with state offices.

At the time of its construction in 1878, this was the largest and highest adobe structure in Santa Fe. Originally there was a third story, destroyed by fire in the 1920s, that served as the college dormitory. The surviving stories of the building housed administrative offices and class-rooms.

The Christian Brothers founded the college in different quarters in 1859, on instructions from Bishop Lamy, as a school for boys, providing formal secondary and college education for the first time in the area. In 1947 the Broth-ers separated the high school and college levels, establish-ing the College of Santa Fe and St. Michael's High School, both now located in other areas of town.

New Mexico State Capitol

Farther south on Old Santa Fe Trail is an unusual state capitol, built in 1966. The architects, shunning typical capitol facades, designed the building in the general shape of a Pueblo kiva and then tried to make it look official by adding territorial trim. The result is a little silly, but not inappropriate for much that happens within. The interior offers little of interest, but the grounds are well-land-scaped and serve as the site for contemporary sculpture displays arranged by the Governor's Gallery.

The "Oldest House" (215 East De Vargas)

Pueblo Indians may have laid the original foundations for this building in the thirteenth century, though the vigas in the current ceiling, according to tree-ring specimens, go back to only about 1750. Whatever the original build-ing date, and whatever the accuracy of the claim to being "the oldest house in the United States," the western por-tion is a good example of old adobe construction. Most Santa Fe residents lived in similar rooms in the early centu-ries, part Indian and part Spanish in architecture, with low, log ceilings, dirt floors, thick adobe walls and a corner fireplace for heating and cooking. The walls are made of poured mud instead of adobe bricks, a once-typical technique called "puddling."

The house is open to visitors free of charge during the business hours of the adjoining gift shop, usually 10:00 to 5:00 daily.

Boyle House (327 East De Vargas)

The Boyle family acquired the house in the 1880s in two different purchases. For some years previous, ownership of the house had been divided between two families, sepa-rated by a central hallway. At various times before then, the house belonged to the Catholic Church, U.S. soldiers and a family of prominent Spanish landowners.

The age of the building is unknown; it is probably as old as most of the structure of the "oldest house." It existed for certain by the 1760s, and the four-foot-thick walls suggest the possibility of an earlier origin. It is still a private residence.

José Alarid House (338 East De Vargas)

José Alarid, a disabled veteran, built this house in the late years of Mexican rule in Santa Fe. He sold the property in 1854, and it changed hands a number of times after that. Bishop Lamy owned the house for five years, though he probably never lived in it.

A later owner, Anita Chapman, was the first woman to serve as territorial librarian. Her immediate successors in the office were also women, which caused a legal controversy in the early part of this century. Ultimately the state Supreme Court had to decide whether a woman could serve in a public position in New Mexico. In a split decision, the court ruled that the office of librarian did not require "judgment in any respect," and so the duties were "not incompatible with the ability of a woman to perform."

Adolph Bandelier House (352 East De Vargas)

Across Paseo de Peralta from the Alarid House is the home Adolph Bandelier rented during his ten-year stay in Santa Fe in the 1880s. Bandelier, an internationally known Swiss scholar, was the first outsider to understand the historical and anthropological significance of the Santa Fe area and to write about it for other outsiders. His research on the Pueblos, which involved living in Indian villages for weeks at a time and traveling thousands of miles on foot and horseback, resulted in a novel called *The Delight Makers*. He wrote scientific papers as well, but had the good sense to realize that his findings were only tentative and best expressed as fiction. The novel is ponderous but definitely worth reading for its imaginative insights about the early Pueblos.

Later owners of the house may be better known locally than Bandelier. Santa Fe merchant Henry Kaune, whose

wife was Bandelier's niece, bought it in 1919. The Kaunes
established a popular local grocery in Santa Fe that is still
thriving today. The house remains a private residence.

A few hundred feet north of the Bandelier House, Paseo
de Peralta crosses over the Santa Fe River. Going west
along the river on Alameda leads back to our starting
point on Old Santa Fe Trail. One block north is the Loretto Chapel.

Loretto Chapel (219 Old Santa Fe Trail)

The Sisters of Loretto built the Chapel of Our Lady of
Light in the 1870s to serve the girls' school they operated
on the present site of the Inn at Loretto. When the boys
of St. Michael's College, right down the street, were wor-
shiping at the Chapel of San Miguel, the girls of Loretto
Academy were here.

The small Gothic chapel, modeled on St. Chapelle in
Paris, was designed by one of the French architects who
was building St. Francis Cathedral at the same time. John
Lamy, nephew of the bishop, shot and killed the architect,
on suspicion of adultery with Lamy's wife, before the
plans were completed. The construction crew could not
figure out how the architect intended to build a stairway
to the choir loft, since there did not seem to be room for
it. They built a loft but finished the job without providing
any means of reaching it.

The nuns were distressed and prayed for the help of
St. Joseph, a carpenter by trade. Before long a carpenter
appeared and constructed the circular "miraculous staircase" without using nails or any visible means of support.
Local legend attributes the work to St. Joseph because the
carpenter disappeared, without pay or even thanks, as
soon as he completed his masterpiece.

The chapel is open from 9:00 to 4:30 daily. There is a
small admission fee.

Chapter Six
♦♦♦♦♦♦♦♦♦
Canyon Road Rambling

C ANYON ROAD is one of the most romantic and picturesque streets in the United States, and certainly the oldest one still in use. The Pueblo Indians established it as a trail at least a century before any Europeans arrived to stay in the Americas. The trail, which ran the same course as the current paved street, followed the Santa Fe River over the Sangre de Cristo Mountains to the Pecos Pueblo. The Spanish conquistadores maintained the route, calling it *el camino de Cañón.*

By the early eighteenth century the Spanish were building homes and cultivating fields along Canyon Road. Sections of some of the current buildings date from this period, when the style of the street's architecture was established in a way that has not changed substantially since. The old adobes that line the narrow, winding street are almost flush with the pavement, giving the walker at some points the feeling of being channeled through an adobe tunnel.

The plain facades along the street present a deceptive impression about what is inside. Residents built the homes

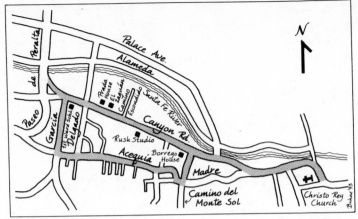

A Walking Tour of Canyon Road and Acequia Madre

around a central patio, or *placita*. As families grew and children started their own families, they added new rooms and separate buildings around the *placita*, producing rambling structures and compounds that are only partially visible from the street. Since the patio was the center of family and social life, landscaping was reserved for that area, and the finest architectural details face inwardly around it, blocked from the dust and noise of the street by the front facade. Twentieth-century American settlers in Santa Fe, unable to give up front yards altogether, modified the style on nearby streets by building freestanding adobe walls right up to the pavement, creating a similar sense of hidden charm.

Early this century Canyon Road became the center of the Santa Fe art colony. Not as many artists live and work there today as in the past—rents are high—but the neighborhood has retained its artistic character. City zoning designates it as a "residential arts and crafts zone," limiting its use to residences, studios, art galleries, crafts shops, restaurants and related neighborhood services. It's an ideal place for exploring both the residential character of the old city and the work of Southwestern artists.

First Ward School Building (400 Canyon Road)

The difficulty that modern ways have encountered in Santa Fe is aptly illustrated in this structure. When it was built in 1906, it was a symbol of progress in two important respects. For one thing, it was constructed with kilned bricks rather than adobe blocks. The bricks were standardized and regular in form, unlike the adobes, and much easier to maintain, which seemed at the time to give them destiny's edge. Also, the city erected the building as a public school, which municipal leaders expected to rapidly displace the existing church schools established by Bishop Lamy. Neither expectation was fulfilled. Some of Lamy's schools are still thriving and brick is even less common today in Santa Fe than at the turn of the century.

The Board of Education sold the building in 1928. Since then it has been a theatre for foreign films, a residence, an antique shop and once even a zoo for indigenous birds and animals. Today it serves modernity again, more successfully, as the home of the Linda Durham Gallery.

Juan José Prada House (519 Canyon Road)

Early maps of Santa Fe indicate this house existed before the Boston Tea Party, though written records go back only to the years right after the Civil War. In the 1860s, when the house was the residence of Juan José Prada, it was divided into two sections separated by a central corridor. Prada sold the west section in 1869, and his widow deeded the east section to her daughter and son-in-law in 1882. Both deeds stipulated that the front door of the corridor, facing the street, be left open for access to a dance hall in the rear of the house.

The dance hall was gone when Mrs. Charles Dietrich purchased the property about 50 years ago and joined the two sections. One of the pioneers of historic preservation in Santa Fe, Mrs. Dietrich lived in the house for many years and was instrumental in saving other old Canyon Road homes from destruction. The building is still a private residence.

Behind the house is one of the few surviving examples of the New Mexico equivalent of the frontier log cabin. From the earliest Spanish days inhabitants used *jacal* construction for some purposes, particularly for outbuildings. The small barn on the Prada property is typical, with squared-off cedar logs set upright in the ground and the cracks filled with adobe. Jacal buildings could be as solid and well-insulated as most log cabins, but they were seldom used as residences because of the superior protection provided by thick adobe walls.

El Zaguán (545 Canyon Road)

This rambling old hacienda is one of the architectural treasures of Santa Fe. When James Johnson bought it in 1849, it consisted of two or three rooms, built at an uncertain earlier date with four-foot-thick walls.

Johnson was a prominent merchant in the days of the Santa Fe Trail. He operated a general store on the northeast corner of the plaza, bringing in his merchandise by wagon train across the trail from Missouri. Behind the house, he built large corrals for the oxen and horses used on the long trek.

Johnson enlarged the house considerably and converted it to territorial style, noticeable from the street by the brick coping on the roof. The new rooms, with walls only three feet thick, included a private chapel, a library that contained the largest collection of books in New Mexico at the time, and a "chocolate room," where chocolate was ground and served each afternoon. At one point there were 24 rooms, even with the servants quartered across the street. As the house grew, so did its *zaguán*, the covered passageway that runs its full length in the back and has given the house its name.

Adolph Bandelier, the pioneering anthropologist, designed the garden west of the house in the 1880s. The two chestnut trees, which have become city landmarks, were already there at the time, but Bandelier brought in the peony bushes from China that are still flourishing a hundred years later.

Among the buildings saved from destruction by Mrs. Charles Dietrich in the 1920s and 1930s, El Zaguán is now owned by the Historic Santa Fe Foundation. Inside, the house has been converted into rental apartments of various sizes, but the exterior has been preserved.

Olive Rush Studio (630 Canyon Road)

Olive Rush was well-known as an artist within the Society of Friends (the Quakers). The first woman to join the budding art colony, she visited Santa Fe in 1914 and moved to the town in 1920.

Rush made her home and studio in this old adobe, which had been in the Seña and Rodríguez families for generations. Judging by the thickness of the walls, the house was probably built in the first half of the nineteenth century. Records from those days are not very informative; there were no surveys and deeds were seldom filed. Families held the same property for generations and knew its boundaries by birthright.

Rush preserved the house in its original state. The Society of Friends, which now uses it as a meeting house, has maintained it with the same degree of care.

Borrego House (724 Canyon Road)

This is one of the few houses on Canyon Road whose history can be traced with Spanish deeds. A smaller version of the house existed in 1753, when it was sold as part of a farm. The farm, like others nearby, extended south from the street a few hundred yards to the *acequia madre*, the source of irrigation water.

The Borrego family owned the home for 75 years during the nineteenth century. They added the large front room, for political and social entertaining, and the territorial-style portal along the street. They also left posterity some incredible deed tangles. The original purchaser, Rafael Borrego, willed half of the property to his widow and half to his children. From then until 1939, various parts of the house were owned by different people, sometimes not of the same family. By the time Rafael's widow died in 1872, the Borregos were deeding individual rooms, a fairly common practice in Santa Fe before the twentieth century. There were even cases where parts of a room were bequeathed to heirs.

Mrs. Charles Dietrich purchased all of the rooms between 1928 and 1939 and restored the house carefully. The property has changed ownership several times since then, but it has been used as a restaurant for many years now.

Camino del Monte Sol

The street just beyond the Borrego House, Camino del Monte Sol, is almost as famous for its artists as Canyon Road. Los Cinco Pintores (the Five Painters), along with several other painters and writers, built homes on the *camino* early in this century. Before then the undeveloped street was called Telephone Road, but the artists found the designation offensive and renamed it after a nearby mountain.

One block along Camino del Monte Sol is Acequia Madre, which is a pleasant street to follow back toward downtown. There is, however, another important sight a few blocks farther up Canyon Road.

Cristo Rey Church

The church houses the most famous piece of Spanish colonial art in New Mexico, an ornately carved stone *reredos*, or altar screen, commissioned in 1760. Originally made for the military chapel, La Castrense, which once stood on the plaza, the *reredos* became a model for many later hand-hewn wooden altar screens in New Mexico. Depicted on the intricate baroque monolith, from top to bottom and left to right, are God, Our Lady of Valvanera, St. John Nepomuk, St. James the Apostle, St. Joseph, St. Ignatius Loyola and St. Francis of Solano.

The church was built in 1940 to commemorate the 400th anniversary of Coronado's expedition into New Mexico. Architect John Gaw Meem designed it in classical Spanish mission style. Nearly two hundred thousand adobe bricks were used in the construction, all made from the soil on the site, as is the traditional practice. Parishioners, working under professional supervision, contributed much of the labor.

Meem scaled the church, one of the largest adobe structures in existence, to fit the great *reredos*. After La Castrense was demolished, Bishop Lamy concealed the altar screen behind a wall in the cathedral. The French prelate disliked local religious art, particularly in his Romanesque church. Meem gave the work a much more proper home.

Cristo Rey is open to visitors from the early morning to the early evening free of charge.

Acequia Madre

The only remaining *acequia*, or irrigation ditch, in Santa Fe is the *acequia madre*—"mother ditch"—which flows along the street that bears its name and is still used to water gardens and trees near its path. Before Santa Fe knew the technology of deep wells and running water, the *acequias* were an essential part of the town's life. They carried melting snow from the mountains into the fields and orchards of the village during the growing season, when rainfall was undependable. Without the *acequias* the area would have been uninhabitable. They remain a cherished and practical part of life along Acequia Madre and north of Santa Fe in rural areas and small towns.

The Pueblos used ditch irrigation at least a thousand years ago, but the Spanish introduced the elaborate irrigation code that still prevails today. Land ownership along an *acequia* provides rights to shares of water from the ditch. Larger fields get larger proportions of the water. Generally water rights are transferred along with land, but owners can lose their rights by not contributing adequately to the maintenance of the ditch. The annual cleaning of the ditches, supervised by the *mayordomo de la acequia*, often remains an important community activity. Everyone with water rights works together to clear the ditch of winter debris from its source down to the last farm.

Acequia Madre dead-ends at Paseo de Peralta, which leads back to the beginning of Canyon Road. For pedestrians, however, a better way to return to the tour's starting point is along tree-lined Garcia Street, one block before the Paseo.

Chapter Seven

♦♦♦♦♦♦♦♦♦♦♦

Museums

EVEN people who avoid museums in other cities should make an exception in Santa Fe. Both the Palace of the Governors and the Museum of Fine Arts would be worth touring even if they were empty. The Museum of International Folk Art, the best institution of its kind in the world, is full of joy, and the several superb collections of Southwestern Indian art are full of elemental energy. For studious sightseeing or just visual delight, Santa Fe's museums should not be missed.

The Palace of the Governors, the Museum of Fine Arts, the Museum of International Folk Art and the Museum of Indian Arts and Culture are all state institutions, required by the legislature to charge admission. The fee for each is $3.50 for adults, but you can get two-day ($6) and annual ($25) passes that allow you to come and go at all four places, a much better value. Children under 16 are free.

Museum of International Folk Art

The most fascinating of the state institutions is the Museum of International Folk Art. The collection is particularly strong in regional Spanish work, but it also encompasses European decorative arts, Latin American crafts, and toys, jewelry and costumes from all ends of the earth.

Florence Dibell Bartlett established the museum in 1953 to house her collection. The acquisition in the early 1980s of the Girard collection—over 106,000 pieces of folk art gathered around the world by Alexander and Susan Girard—firmly solidified the museum's international leadership in its field. Mr. Girard designed a long-standing exhibition of some of the pieces that will astonish and amuse children and adults alike.

The 1989 opening of the Hispanic Heritage Wing considerably expanded the facilities, allowing the museum to showcase more regional art and to present a regular schedule of demonstrations, workshops and performances. With the collection's depth in traditional Hispanic art, the shows in the new wing are usually extraordinary.

The museum is located on Camino Lejo, just off Old Santa Fe Trail, about two miles south of the plaza. It is open daily, except Monday in the winter, from 10:00 to 4:45. Call 505/827-6350 for additional information.

Museum of Indian Arts and Culture

The newest state museum, opened in 1986, exhibits work formerly housed with the older Laboratory of Anthropology. The Laboratory was established in 1931 to preserve and protect the Indian heritage of New Mexico. Before land can be developed in the state, the Laboratory has to certify through archaeological research that the site does not have historical significance. The Laboratory is also entrusted with the care of Indian art and artifacts belonging to the state. The Museum of Indian Arts and Culture now presents this bountiful collection to the public and provides interpretive exhibitions on the prehistory and ethnology of Southwestern Indians.

The museum is located on Camino Lejo, adjacent to the Museum of International Folk Art, about two miles south of the plaza. It is open daily, except Monday in the winter, from 10:00 to 4:45. The phone number is 505/ 827-6344.

Wheelwright Museum of the American Indian

Mary Cabot Wheelwright founded this private museum in 1937 to help preserve disappearing aspects of Navajo religion and ceremony. When the Navajos took up their own preservation efforts, much of the original collection was returned to them and the scope of the museum was broadened. Exhibits today feature American Indian arts and artifacts from any period or place. The museum shop downstairs, designed to resemble an old Navajo trading post, is almost as large and interesting as the exhibition area. For family fun in the summer, catch the tales of storyteller Joe Hayes, presented outdoors on the grounds; call 505/982-4636 for dates and times.

The Wheelwright is on Camino Lejo, behind the Museum of International Folk Art, about two miles south of the plaza. It is open Monday through Saturday 10:00 to 5:00 and Sunday 1:00 to 5:00. Donations are requested.

Palace of the Governors

Described in Chapter 4, the Palace is an ideal spot for its exhibitions on New Mexico history. It also houses an extensive historical library, a photo archive and a collection of manuscripts that go back to the seventeenth century. One of the museum's main annual events is the popular Mountain Man Rendezvous and Buffalo Roast, usually scheduled for the second week of August. The period costumes, trade fair and entertainment make it a special evening even if your appetite isn't fixed on buffalo, *cabrito* (goat) or Rio Grande catfish stew. Call 505/827-6474 for dates and ticket information.

Part of the Museum of New Mexico, the Palace is open daily, except Monday in the winter, from 10:00 to 4:45. It's located on the central plaza.

Museum of Fine Arts

Also described in Chapter 4, the Museum of Fine Arts features twentieth-century paintings, prints, sculpture and photography from New Mexico. Not all of the exhibits are regional, but most have some direct connection to the state. Many of the shows come from the museum's 8,000-piece collection, which was recently enhanced with the acquisition of several important Georgia O'Keeffe paintings that the artist kept for her own enjoyment until her death.

Located next to the Palace of the Governors, just off the plaza, the museum is open daily, except Monday in the winter, from 10:00 to 4:45. Call 505/827-4455 for additional information.

Center for Contemporary Arts

In the last decade the Center for Contemporary Arts has displaced the Museum of Fine Arts as the advocate and exhibition space for contemporary artists living in the community. The Center also presents shows from elsewhere, particularly ones featuring high-quality out-of-the-mainstream art, and regularly brings in artists and film-makers from across the country to demonstrate and discuss their work. The film series operated by the private, non-profit organization is one of the best in the United States for avant-garde cinema. The gallery is open Tuesday through Friday 9:00 to 4:00 and Saturday 12:00 to 4:00, but many events are scheduled in the evening. Call 505/982-1338 for details.

The Center is at 291 E. Barcelona, near the intersection with Old Pecos Trail. Admission to the gallery is free; charges for other events vary.

Old Cienega Village Museum

The Old Cienega Village Museum is part of El Rancho de las Golondrinas, the Ranch of the Swallows, a large, well-restored Spanish colonial estate on the outskirts of Santa Fe. A private foundation maintains the operating ranch as a living museum of the Spanish colonial heritage.

The ranch includes houses built in the seventeenth and eighteenth centuries, farm buildings, blacksmithing and wheelwright facilities, several water mills and a winery. Don't miss the interesting re-creation of an old Spanish mountain village, typical of rural life north of Santa Fe in earlier years, and the *morada*, a special kind of chapel used by *penitentes*.

The ranch is open for self-guided tours Wednesday through Sunday in June, July and August from 10:00 to 4:00. There are guided tours Monday through Saturday in June, July and August at 10:00 A.M. Groups can arrange special tours at other times between April 1 and October 31 by calling 505/473-4169 well in advance.

The best times to visit are during the spring and fall festivals, usually held on the first weekends of June and October. On these occasions local Spanish artists demonstrate colonial crafts and perform traditional folk music and dances. On festival weekends there is not a more fascinating place in the area.

El Rancho is located in La Cienega, which can be reached by an exit off Interstate 25, a few miles south of the Santa Fe city limits. There is a $3 admission charge for adults ($1–$2 for children), which goes up about $2 per person on festival weekends. The general information number is 505/471-2261.

School of American Research

The School of American Research has been an important force in Santa Fe life for most of the twentieth century. The Archaeological Institute of America established it as a research center in 1907 to further the study of American prehistory. Anthropologists working at the school contributed considerably to early local and national interest in the Southwestern heritage, encouraging preservation efforts and the growth of tourism.

A major force in the development of the Museum of New Mexico, the School was housed for many years in the Palace of the Governors. In 1972 it moved to its present headquarters in a lovely residential compound at 660 E. Garcia Street.

The school's outstanding collection of Southwestern Indian art can be seen only on special tours, normally scheduled on Friday at 2:00. The cost is $15. Call 505/982-3584 for a reservation.

Institute of American Indian Arts

Primarily an art school for Native American students, the Institute has trained many prominent Indian artists, including Dan Namingha, Doug Hyde, Barry Coffin and Earl Biss. The faculty has been equally notable, ranging

from sculptor Allan Houser to jewelry artist Charles Lo-
loma. With this kind of talent in residence, the Institute
accumulated a wonderfully diverse collection of modern
Indian work. Some of the eight thousand pieces are on
permanent display in the renovated old Federal Building
downtown, across from St. Francis Cathedral at 108 Cathedral Place. Hours are Monday through Saturday from
9:00 to 6:00, Wednesday evenings until 8:00 and Sunday
from noon to 5:00. Admission is $3.50 for adults and $2
for children over 5. Call 505/988-6281 for additional
information.

Randall Davey Audubon Center

No single place can represent the totality of the Santa Fe
heritage, but the Randall Davey house and educational
center comes close. Once a Spanish land grant, later the
site of a U.S. Army sawmill, then the home and studio of
one of the early leaders of the local art colony, the expansive estate offers a little of everything. You can tour the
historic home, which was originally the mill, see Davey's
art, and learn about the flora and fauna of northern New
Mexico on nature trails through the Audubon Center's
wilderness area. The staff organizes and presents a series
of natural history workshops, bird walks and other activities.

The Randall Davey Audubon Center is at the end of
Upper Canyon Road. It's open daily from 9:00 to 5:00,
except weekends from December through March, for a
small donation. The phone number is 505/983-4609.

Santa Fe Children's Museum

The Santa Fe Children's Museum features hands-on, par-
ticipatory exhibits in the arts, humanities and sciences.
The facility is small, but the atmosphere of discovery is

exciting and the program of workshops, demonstrations and performances is ambitious.

At 1050 Old Pecos Trail, around the corner from the Center for Contemporary Arts, the museum is open from 10:00 to 5:00 Thursday through Saturday and noon to 5:00 on Sunday all year. During the summer, the museum opens on Wednesdays as well. Admission is $1 for kids under 12 and $2 for anyone older. Call 505/989-8359 for additional information.

Chapter Eight
◆◆◆◆◆◆◆◆◆◆◆◆

North to Taos

WHEN the Spanish arrived in New Mexico to stay in the seventeenth century, some of the more independent and adventurous settlers pushed on beyond Santa Fe to the north. They established farms on both sides of the Rio Grande Valley, all along the 75-mile stretch between Santa Fe and the large Indian pueblo in Taos. Santa Fe was a small, isolated frontier village in this period, but compared to the northern settlements it was a busy, cosmopolitan metropolis. A common punishment for crimes in the early centuries was banishment to one or another of these remote villages, where life was invariably hard and lean.

Santa Fe courts no longer exile convicts to Chimayó or Las Trampas, but little else has changed substantially in these places. If anything, survival may be tougher today in the northern villages than it was in the seventeenth and eighteenth centuries, and the villages have certainly lost ground to Santa Fe in contact with the outside world. Taos is, and always has been, a special case among the northern communities, but the others remain frontier out-

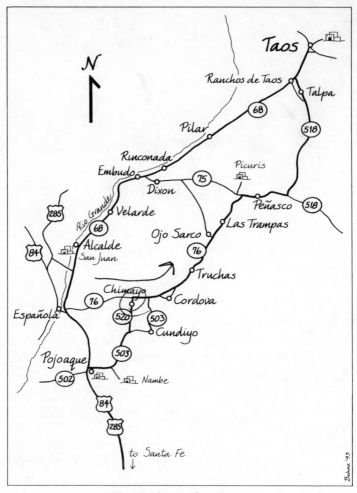

The High Road to Taos

posts of the Old World, rustic, pastoral and still thoroughly Spanish.

Two superb books provide wonderful insights into the villages' confrontation with "progress." Robert Coles describes the persistence of their traditional values and mores in *The Old Ones of New Mexico* (Harcourt Brace

Jovanovich, 1989). Taos writer John Nichols creates a fictional but authentic mountain community, populated with splendid characters, in the delightful *The Milagro Beanfield War* (Ballantine, 1987), translated to film by Robert Redford in 1988.

The "high road" to Taos from Santa Fe, depicted on the map, passes through several of the Old World villages described in this chapter. Definitely take this route north unless the roads are icy. The mountain scenery is spectacular, but the towns along the way are the real treat. The main highway between the two cities, which follows the old Camino Real, is also interesting and scenic at points, a good way to return to Santa Fe.

Chimayó

Chimayó, the center of Spanish weaving in New Mexico, is the first town of note along the high road. Families such as the Ortegas and the Trujillos have been weaving in Chimayó for centuries. Many years ago they developed a design pattern, named for the village, that is characterized by a background of one solid color with stylized diamond figures in the center and stripes on the ends in different colors.

A good place to see examples of the weaving today is at the Ortega family shop, where artisans work daily at their looms. The Ortegas stopped using homespun yarn in the 1930s, and they now employ some weavers from outside of the family, but the essence of their craft hasn't changed much since the eighteenth century. The Trujillo family shop, Centinela Weavers, features excellent work by Irvin Trujillo, his wife Lisa, and other fine artisans from the area.

The major attraction in Chimayó is El Santuario de Nuestro Señor de Esquípulas, a small chapel that is one of the most revered places in the Southwest. The facade and the religious folk art inside are simple and unpolished, but intensely expressive, typical of Spanish frontier churches of the early nineteenth century.

The ground on which the chapel is built is reputed to have miraculous healing powers. Pilgrims visit Chimayó as they do Lourdes in France, to cure their afflictions through faith. In a tiny back room they crouch over a hole in the middle of the floor and scoop up holy earth to rub over their arms and faces. In an adjoining room many of the cured have left their crutches, leg braces and other testimonies of their faith.

Other kinds of pilgrims look for their succor at the Rancho de Chimayó, one of the best-known restaurants in New Mexico. Housed in a lovely adobe hacienda, not far from the Santuario, the Rancho serves some of the most authentic traditional cooking in the state. If you prefer a quick, casual meal or snack, Léona's de Chimayó, a stand next door to the Santuario, offers hearty and delicious tamales and other native dishes. Léona's flour tortillas may be the best in the country.

Cordova

Cordova is a few miles east of Chimayó, just off the high road in a heavily tilled valley. It is known primarily for its woodcarving, particularly a style—named for the village—of carefully incised, unpainted *santos*.

The founder of the modern carving tradition in Cordova was José Dolores López, born in 1868. Like his father before him, López was a carpenter and furniture maker by trade who used his skills in his free time to help beautify the local church. During World War I, anxious about a son who had been drafted, López began carving small wooden figures, mainly animals, for relaxation. Members of the Santa Fe art colony "discovered" his work shortly afterwards and convinced López that he should begin making some carvings to sell, which must have been a startling idea in Cordova at the time. López taught his techniques to his children, including the talented George López, who the National Endowment for the Arts has honored as a national treasure. George and his siblings passed along the tradition to their children, including Sabanita Ortiz, Gloria López Cordova and Eluid L. Martinez.

The local artists welcome visitors to their homes to see and buy carvings. Just follow the hand-lettered signs in the village.

Truchas, Las Trampas and Peñasco

Truchas, the next community along the high road, has magnificent views across miles of mountain and desert. Another center of New Mexico weaving, Truchas is known for a design scheme that varies a little from the Chimayó style. Local weavers, such as the Cordova family, often use a pattern called Vallero, developed about a century ago by the Montoya sisters in the nearby town of El Valle. Other fine crafts are showcased at Hand Artes Gallery, and an ambitious selection of contemporary paintings, drawings and sculpture can be seen at Cardona-Hine Gallery, both found along the village's main road.

For sustenance, try breakfast, lunch or dinner at the Romero family's Truchas Mountain Cafe. The stuffed sopaipillas and other local fare are first-rate. While you're there, ask directions to the meadow nearby that served as the beanfield in Robert Redford's film version of *The Milagro Beanfield War*, which was shot in Truchas and used many residents as extras. Two rustically charming bed-and-breakfast inns provide lodging for those who want to explore at length. Contact the Truchas Farmhouse B&B at 505/689-2245 or Rancho Arriba at 505/689-2374.

Las Trampas is the site of a beautiful Spanish colonial chapel, San José de Gracias, built in the mid-eighteenth century. The chapel is sometimes open on summer days. When locked, local residents can find the key if you're persistent and respectful. The religious folk art of the interior is superb. Donations are welcome and needed.

At Peñasco the high road goes east several miles along a fertile valley and then turns north for Taos on Route 3. Close to Peñasco is Picuris Pueblo, founded in the late thirteenth century. One of the more pleasant pueblos to visit, Picuris has a small museum, ancient ruins and even a campground.

Ranchos de Taos

The high road connects with Highway 68, the main route between Santa Fe and Taos, in the town of Ranchos de Taos, home of one of the most photographed churches in the United States. Though the St. Francis of Assisi Mission is a small chapel, it has massive adobe walls and buttresses that cast grand shadows in the New Mexico sun.

The small plaza around the church offers low-key local character, but that spirit disappears as you head north along the road into Taos. Don't be discouraged by this section of Route 68, a franchise strip much like Santa Fe's Cerrillos Road. Within a few miles you reach the Taos central plaza.

Taos Plaza and Downtown

The Spanish founded Taos around the plaza in 1617 and it has been the center of community life ever since. Though the area now brims with souvenir shops, there are numerous points of interest, both historic and contemporary, in the neighborhood.

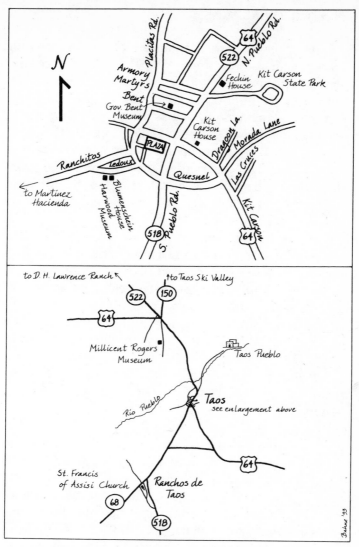

Taos (above) and Vicinity (below)

Directly on the plaza, La Fonda Hotel has an amazing collection of erotic paintings by D. H. Lawrence, displayed in the manager's office for a small admission. You can see tamer W.P.A. murals across the street at Burke Armstrong Fine Arts, as well as paintings from the same era and later. New Directions Gallery, also on the plaza, features work by contemporary artists from the area, some nationally recognized. At the east end of the plaza, check out the bantam downtown branch of the Millicent Rogers Museum (see page 82) and the museum-quality Maison-Faurie Antiquités shop.

Several other museums and historic homes nearby offer glimpses into the Taos past in a more accessible way than similar places in Santa Fe. East of the plaza one block is the home of Taos's best-known resident, Kit Carson. The famous scout, whose life was romanticized in the dime novels of the nineteenth century, bought the house as a wedding gift for his wife, Josefa, and lived here for 24 years. Don't confuse the souvenir shop directly on the street with the home's gift shop, which is off the rear patio and is an excellent source of Southwestern reading material.

The Carson Home (505/758-0505) is open as a museum daily, 8:00 to 6:00 in the summer and 9:00 to 5:00 in the winter. Admission is $3 for adults and $2 for children. Consider a combination ticket that includes visits to the Ernest L. Blumenschein Home and Martinez Hacienda, a fine value for three of the most fascinating spots in town. Taos Walking Tours (505/758-4020) leave from the Carson Home daily at 10:00, June through September, for a behind-the-scenes overview of the downtown area. The cost is $10.

Charles Bent, the first U.S. territorial governor of New Mexico, lived one block north of the plaza before he was killed at home in a local uprising against American rule. Artifacts of the early Southwest are displayed in the house

today, but the tone overall is as commercial as it is historical. Visiting hours are 10:00 to 5:00 daily in the summer
and 10:00 to 4:00 in the winter. Admission is $1 for
adults and half of that for kids over 8. Call 505/758-2376
for additional information.

A little farther north on the main street, at 227 N.
Pueblo Road (Route 68), the home of Russian artist Nico-
lai Fechin dates to the 1920s. Fechin carved the elaborate
woodwork and many of the furnishings. When you see
the intricate detail you'll wonder how he ever had time to
paint. The Fechin Institute (505/758-1710) holds periodic
workshops and exhibitions, but usually opens the home
to visitors on Wednesdays through Sundays from 1:00 to
5:30, May through early October. The suggested donation is $3.

The Harwood Foundation Museum and Library (505/
758-9826) is south of the plaza on Ledoux Street. Over-
seen by the University of New Mexico, the museum has
an extensive collection of paintings by founders of the
Taos art colony as well as Spanish crafts from the area.
It is open free Monday to Friday 12:00 to 5:00 and 10:00
to 4:00 on Saturday.

One of the best-known painters represented in the Harwood collection, Ernest Blumenschein, lived two doors
down Ledoux Street. The rambling old adobe home, dating to 1797, blends worldly sophistication and Taos sim-
plicity in its period furnishings. No place else provides
such insight into the early decades of the local art colony.
You can tour Blumy's residence (505/758-0505) daily,
9:00 to 5:00. Admission is $3 for adults and $2 for children.

While on tiny Ledoux Street, stop in at Collins-Pettit
Gallery, which handles contemporary figurative work, or
at other galleries in the same compound. On the way back
to the plaza, Clay and Fiber (126 W. Plaza Drive) carries
a solid collection of fine crafts.

Other downtown galleries worthy of a serious look include Mission Gallery (138 E. Kit Carson), DEL Fine Arts (109 E. Kit Carson), and the Stables Gallery (133 N. Pueblo Road). A longer hike, or a quick drive, will take you to Lumina (239 Morada), a gallery of contemporary photography and painting in a historic home. Twining Weavers (208 Ranchitos Road), a little farther from downtown, offers a production line of fine fabrics.

Taos Pueblo

The most impressive place in Taos may be the pueblo, a few miles north of the plaza. Virtually unchanged in appearance since the Spanish first saw it, it is the best preserved and most striking of all the Indian pueblos in New Mexico.

Some of the residents continue to live in one of the two enormous adobe communal buildings, divided into many separate rooms, that reach five stories into the sky. The mountain creek that runs between the two apartment compounds flows from sacred Blue Lake, high in the surrounding mountains. The river provides water for the ancient dwellings, which have no plumbing or electricity to this day.

Visitors are allowed to wander through the central section of the pueblo, where some people open their homes as tourist shops. Large "Restricted" signs keep visitors well away from the kivas. There is a $5 parking fee, a $5 fee for using a still camera and a $10 fee for using a movie camera. The Taos Indian Horse Ranch (505/758-3212) provides guided trail rides across pueblo land beyond the village. Rates vary depending on the size of the group and the length of the ride but run around $50 to $65 per adult for 2 hours.

Taos Ski Valley

The Taos Ski Valley is north and east of town about 30 minutes, surrounded by the majestic Carson National Forest. Even if you're not a skier, a winter visit can be an exhilarating experience. Founded by a true pioneer of the sport, the late Ernie Blake, the area exudes Alpine ambience.

Expert skiers love the wide variety of challenging runs, the bowl skiing and the great powder, and the less-skilled have plenty of alternatives among the 70-plus runs. The ski school is first-rate and sometimes an incredible value; sign up for group lessons on a weekday morning during a non-holiday period and you may end up with a private or semiprivate lesson for a bargain price. If you're not skiing, you can still enjoy lunch below the slopes, have a toddy or hot chocolate, bask in the winter sun and watch the hotdoggers schuss down Al's Run. A handful of inns are located at the base (see "Lodging," below). Call 505/776-2291 for Taos Ski Valley information and 505/776-2916 for snow conditions.

Other Taos Attractions

The other major sights of Taos are farther from the plaza. West of town on Route 240 (Ranchitos Road), the Martinez Hacienda (505/758-0505) is one of the few remaining Spanish Colonial homes open to the public. The fortress-like hacienda, built in 1780 by Severino Martinez, served as a trade center and a refuge from raiding Comanches and Apaches. Today it houses exhibitions on Spanish culture and traditions in northern New Mexico. Definitely worth the short drive, the hacienda welcomes visitors from 9:00 to 5:00 daily. Admission is $3 for adults and $2 for children.

The Millicent Rogers Museum and the D. H. Lawrence Ranch and Shrine are north of town, beyond the pueblo. The Millicent Rogers (505/758-2462) has an outstanding collection of Southwestern Indian and Spanish art and a great shop, too. Many visitors miss it because of the rather isolated location—about one-half mile west of Route 522, near the intersection with the road to the ski basin—but the museum is one of the best in the region. It is open daily 9:00 to 5:00. Admission is $3 for adults and $1 for kids.

The D. H. Lawrence Ranch is about fifteen miles farther, at the end of a scenic but rough mountain road that connects to Route 522. The road, which should not be attempted in poor weather, is unnumbered, but small signs along it and Route 522 point the way. The ranch is now owned by the University of New Mexico, which uses it as a retreat center. The only area open to the public is Lawrence's shrine, a simple monument where his ashes are interred.

Lawrence would have enjoyed Taos's annual Poetry Circus, one of the liveliest literary events in the country. Held each June, it will forever obliterate images of poetry readings as dull. Call 505/758-1029 for details. The Taos Summer Chamber Music Festival starts the same month and runs until early August. The concerts are at the Taos Community Auditorium downtown and the Taos Ski Valley's delightful Hotel St. Bernard. Phone 505/776-2388 for the schedule and tickets. Music from Angel Fire, run by former Santa Fe Chamber Music Festival personnel, holds several of its late summer concerts in Taos, usually at the end of August or in early September. Call 800/732-8267 or 505/758-4667 for more information.

Lodging

Taos accommodations offer a good measure of charm at prices a shade lower than Santa Fe's for similar comfort.

The best deals occur in the fall and spring. (Winter skiing makes Taos as popular in the cold months as in the summer.) The rates listed are for the high seasons. Only the bed-and-breakfast inns tend to keep the same prices year-round. Major credit cards are accepted unless noted.

The most enjoyable hotels are the Sagebrush Inn (505/758-2254), on Route 68 a few miles south of the plaza, and the Taos Inn (505/758-2233), in the heart of town on North Pueblo. Both of the moderately priced establishments are loaded with Southwestern character. Georgia O'Keeffe lived and painted for a period in the 1930s at the Sagebrush, built the previous decade with traditional adobe techniques. Rooms start at $82; in the winter it's a good idea to spend an additional $16 to get a fireplace. The lobby bar is the most colorful watering hole in the state and provides live entertainment in the late evening, sometimes featuring name entertainers like Taos resident Michael Martin Murphey.

The Taos Inn was constructed in the nineteenth century as a cluster of separate residences. The town's first physician, Dr. Paul Martin, bought the complex when he moved to Taos in 1895 and his widow converted it to a hotel on his death in 1935. An official National Historic Landmark, it's more likely than the Sagebrush to extend its enchantment into your room. Each of the 40 quarters is different, though most have adobe fireplaces and all are distinctively decorated with Zapotec bedspreads and handmade furniture. Rates range from $80 to $155.

The Quail Ridge Inn (800/624-4448 or 505/776-2211), north of town on the Ski Valley Road, could be a good family option. With condominium accommodations and a country club atmosphere, it's primarily a tennis resort and conference center. The facilities include six outdoor and two indoor tennis courts, four racquetball courts, saunas, hot tubs and a heated pool that is covered in the winter. Nightly rates run from $85 for two people in a

condo bedroom only to $220 for up to six folks in a full
two-bedroom apartment. The condominiums are more
luxurious at Hacienda de Valdez (505/776-2218), a newer
development about halfway between town and the Taos
Ski Valley. Expect to pay $230 to $275 for quarters large
enough for six to eight people.

At the Taos Ski Valley itself, the Hotel St. Bernard (505/
776-2251) and the Hotel Edelweiss (505/776-2301) offer
handsome Alpine-style lodging during the winter. Both
are just a schuss away from the lifts. Unfortunately for
many of us, they usually take only week-long bookings.
If you've got the time and the money, and plan well in
advance, they're the best spots to hang your skis. Rates
of $1,200 to $1,300 per person for seven nights include
most or all meals, ski lessons, lift tickets and many other
amenities. St. Bernard takes no credit cards. Discounted
deals for fewer nights may be available at the very beginning or end of the season, depending on conditions. You
can experience Edelweiss on a more limited scale from
June to November, when it operates as a B&B for $65 a
night. For other ski area lodging information or reservations, contact the Taos Valley Resort Association at 800/
992-7669 or locally at 505/776-2233.

As in Santa Fe, good bed-and-breakfast inns have pro-
liferated in Taos in the last decade. The most luxurious
B&B is Casa de las Chimeneas (505/758-4777). Although
built as a humble two-room adobe in the 1920s, Chimeneas flowered over time into a grand hacienda. Each of the
guest rooms has a fireplace, in keeping with the property's
name, and a private entrance overlooking the formal garden. Mexican tiles, vigas and hand-carved furnishings
contribute to the ambience, and mini-refrigerators and
cable TVs provide modern comforts. The library-style
suite is among the top quarters in the Southwest. Rates
range from about $100 to $150.

The Willows Inn (505/758-2558) is another gem, a

well-designed cluster of rooms surrounding a courtyard in a home that once belonged to artist E. Martin Hennings. You can splurge on Hennings's former studio, which has a private patio, or settle into one of the four other lovely rooms. In either case you'll get a fireplace, vigas, Southwest furniture and loads of charm. Rates run from $80 up to $125.

Two B&Bs occupy parts of the picturesque former estate of the flamboyant Mabel Dodge Luhan (see Chapter 3). Her 200-year-old adobe home is now the Mabel Dodge Luhan House (505/758-9456), less polished than most of our lodging choices but full of personality at rates from $70 to $125. The accommodations are several steps up in contemporary quality at the second option, Hacienda del Sol (505/758-0287). Rates range from $55 to $115 depending on whether you want a private bath, a fireplace, your own steam room or other amenities, though you get excellent value and Southwestern style at all prices. Hacienda del Sol takes credit cards but prefers cash.

If you want to be downtown, try Casa Benevides (137 E. Kit Carson, 505/758-1772) or El Rincon, a block closer to the plaza (110 E. Kit Carson, 505/758-4874). Mainly Victorian in decor, Casa Benevides is the classier of the pair. Rates range from $80 for a simple room with a private bath to $175 for a spacious suite with a full kitchen and private patio. El Rincon is closer to the funky, handmade feel of old Taos. You may find a Balinese fertility goddess hanging over the bed or a bathroom covered floor to ceiling in tiles and murals depicting the Garden of Eden. Most rooms run between $50 and $95.

The Taos Bed and Breakfast Association (800/876-7857 or 505/758-4747) represents Casa de Chimeneas, Hacienda del Sol and other inns, about a dozen collectively. Don't hesitate to take their advice on another B&B if our recommendations are unavailable. If you'd like to stay at a cabin on the banks of the Rio Grande or in an adobe *casita* under the cottonwoods, check with Rio Grande Reservations (800/678-7586 or 505/758-4696). They handle bookings for rural B&Bs near Taos.

Taos has a number of chain motels, but we prefer a couple of renovated old motor courts that have individual style and Southwestern flavor. El Monte (505/758-3171) and the neighboring Adobe Wall (505/758-3972) are east of downtown on Kit Carson Road, resting under the shade of sprawling trees. El Monte's rooms have a range of facilities, from fireplaces to full kitchens, and are priced from $65 up. Abobe Wall starts at $50.

Restaurants

Taos doesn't compare in restaurant quality with Santa Fe, but few towns of 10,000 offer the variety and character found at dining establishments here. The best options are Doc Martin's, the Apple Tree and Brett House, all featuring fresh fish and seafood, fine pasta, inventive variations on regional cooking and charming atmosphere.

At Doc Martin's (505/758-2233), in the Taos Inn on North Pueblo Road, try the turkey enchiladas or the mixed grill with venison, lamb and beef. A good selection of wines are available by the bottle or the glass. The Apple Tree (505/758-1900), a block away in an old adobe at 26 Bent Street, is particularly skilled at trout and vegetarian dishes. At Brett House on the ski basin road (Highway 150 just east of Route 64, 505/776-8545) one of the recent specials we sampled was a robust penne pasta with tomato and goat cheese. All three places serve lunch and dinner. Call ahead for evening reservations at any of them.

La Cigale (505/751-0500), in the Pueblo Alegro strip shopping center on South Pueblo Road, is a newer restaurant with solid potential. The French chef-owner features classic French bistro dishes at lunch and dinner.

Great versions of native New Mexican fare unfortunately are rare. Two of the best bets, El Taoseño (505/758-9511) and Don Pedro's (505/758-9281), are south of the plaza on Pueblo Road. For another version of local flavor, eat at Michael's Kitchen (505/758-4178) on North Pueblo Road, a popular and colorful spot offering a little of everything at decent prices all day.

Dori's (505/758-9222), nearby on the same street, is good for breakfast or just coffee, as is the Mainstreet Bakery (505/758-9610) on Guadalupe Plaza. Bent Street Deli (505/758-5787), named for its location, has tasty sandwiches and salads, a pleasant patio and food to go for mountain picnics or dinner in your hotel room.

The Camino Real to Santa Fe

If you took the high road up to Taos, return to Santa Fe along Route 68, connecting to U.S. 84/285 in Española. The highway follows the route the Spanish colonists used, the old Camino Real.

From Pilar south to Embudo the road parallels the Rio Grande through a scenic gorge. Pilar is a river-rafting center and also the home of the Plum Tree (505/758-4696), a combination country B&B and hostel that sponsors an ambitious series of summer arts workshops.

Embudo Station (505/852-4707), once a stop on the Chile Line railroad, now is a stop for smoked meats and home-brewed beer during the warmer months of the year. You can dangle your toes in the Rio Grande while feasting on trout or baby back ribs washed down with the day's special brew, maybe a green chile beer.

Just east of Embudo, off the highway, is the interesting town of Dixon. Early each November the community hosts a studio tour that includes local farms and La Chirapada winery as well as artists' homes. La Chirapada, open daily throughout the year except on Sundays, makes a blended white wine called Primavera that goes well with the native food.

As the highway leaves the river gorge, you enter a rich agricultural valley. Dixon writer Stanley Crawford, who farms with his wife Rosemary, has penned two insightful accounts of life here, *Mayordomo* (University of New Mexico Press, 1988) and *The Garlic Testament* (HarperCollins, 1992). The area is particularly pleasant in the late summer and early fall, when the highway is lined with fruit and vegetable stands selling bright red chile *ristras* and other local produce. Look for the stand operated by Herman Valdez on the north side of Velarde. His wife Loretta makes distinctive wreaths with dried chiles, gourds, corn and more.

The Spanish village of Alcalde is the site of an unusual dance pageant each Christmas, *Las Matachines*. The traditional dance goes back in Spanish history to the time of the Moors. San Juan Pueblo is just beyond the village.

Española is a little farther south, before the highway turns dull for the last stretch into Santa Fe. It's the largest and most curiously contemporary of the old Hispanic towns in the north. On nights and weekends it becomes a showcase for elaborate "lowrider" cars, a major focus of the community's social life. The customized machines glide down the highway through town an inch or so off the asphalt, moving at a barely discernible pace.

If you're hungry, try Jo Ann's Ranch-o-Casados (505/753-2837), on Highway 68, for good native food from morning to night. The Western-theme dining booths will take you straight back to the 1950s. Of the same vintage, the Stop and Eat Drive-In (505/753-7400), around the corner at 110 S. Oñate, serves pre-franchise burgers and a hearty version of one of New Mexico's favorite fast foods, the Frito pie.

Chapter Nine
♦♦♦♦♦♦♦♦♦♦♦
South to Albuquerque

S PANISH colonists established Albuquerque in 1706, a century after their ancestors settled Santa Fe. The founders named the town for the then Viceroy of New Spain, the Duke of Alburquerque, whose only claim to historic honor comes from the modern city that misspells his once-revered title by dropping the first "r."

Albuquerque remained a small and somnolent village until 1880, when the railroad roared into town. Santa Fe was still much larger at that time, and more of a commercial center, but the capital spurned the Atchison, Topeka, and Santa Fe Railroad, sending the namesake line south instead. That quirk of fate turned Albuquerque into the transportation hub of the state and stimulated a steady growth of industry and population.

The city consolidated its position as New Mexico's urban center in the early decades of the twentieth century. One of the nation's first airlines, TWA, made Albuquerque an overnight stop on its early cross-country flights, and America's "Mother Road," the famed Route 66, brought two generations of highway travelers directly through downtown.

Today Albuquerque is home to a third of the state's population, some four hundred thousand people, but it still feels like a small town in many ways. The combination of old and new, of balmy and bustling, appeals to residents and visitors alike.

Turquoise Trail

Interstate 25 is the quickest way to get between Santa Fe and Albuquerque, but if you can take an extra thirty to sixty minutes, you can make the drive a fascinating journey. Following Highway 14 on the eastern side of the Sandia Mountains, the Turquoise Trail meanders south from Santa Fe's Cerrillos Road through old mining towns, piñon-dotted hills, striking rock formations and mountain vistas. The map of northern New Mexico in the front of the book shows the route.

The first stop of interest, worth a few minutes' detour, is the town of Cerrillos, several hundred yards west of Highway 14. Almost everything was mined here at one time, including gold, silver, lead, zinc and high-quality turquoise. At its peak in the 1880s Cerrillos had 21 bars and four hotels. Today it's a lot more quaint than busy, with a couple of antique and gift shops among abandoned storefronts. The short main street has the look of an old frontier town and has been used as such in movie shoots.

Just beyond Cerrillos is the turnoff to the east for the Iris Ranch, marked by a small sign. The privately owned spread, several miles down a potholed road, grows a stunning array of irises in a profusion of colors, standing out in remarkable contrast to the arid landscape. The flowers generally reach their peak between mid-May and mid-June, when travelers should definitely plan a visit. Call 505/473-3148 for more information.

The next town is Madrid. A coal-mining community founded in the nineteenth century, it once bustled with 3,000 residents, but everyone left after the mines closed following World War II. Madrid was a ghost town from then until its resurgence in the 1970s, when some enterprising artists realized that the coal company's old wood-frame cabins could provide cheap housing. They bought up the one-street town piece by piece and established Madrid as a countercultural center.

Among the several shops now open, Madrid Earthenware Pottery is a good place to check out the work of local artists. If you're looking for a snack instead, head to Maya Jones next door, which has an old soda fountain and Guatemalan imports. The Mine Shaft Tavern will quench a thirst for stronger drink in authentic western-saloon style, but we wouldn't bother with the food. For a midday meal, we usually stick with sandwiches or soup from the Noon Whistle.

In the 1920s over 100,000 people came to Madrid annually during the Christmas season to see the town's display of holiday lights. The glow was so grand on Christmas Eve that airlines would reroute cross-country flights just to pass over it. Today's Christmas show isn't nearly so elaborate, but it still has its allure.

The next burg on the Turquoise Trail is Golden, a withering village that in 1825 was the site of the first gold rush west of the Mississippi. Shortly after Golden, as you approach the Albuquerque metropolitan area, you can take a detour west up to the Sandia Peak Ski Area, where the views are grand year-round. If the idea appeals to you, consider making the trek later from the other side of the mountain, riding up on the Sandia Park Tramway, the world's longest. The skiing facilities and season are limited compared with Santa Fe and Taos, but the slopes attract many beginners and intermediates during the winter.

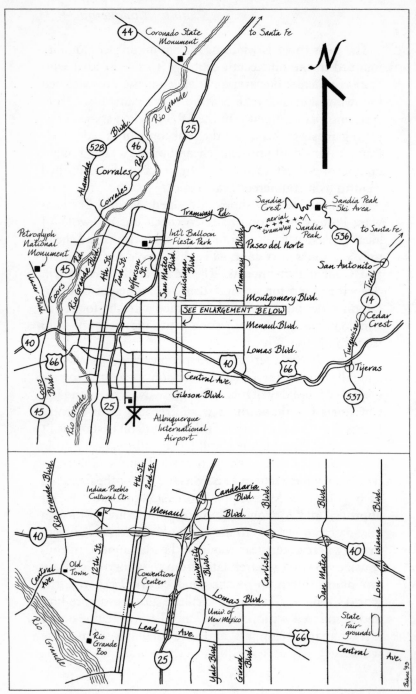

Albuquerque (above) and central Albuquerque (below)

The highway broadens after the turnoff to Sandia Peak and takes you quickly to Interstate 40. Head west from this point toward the city, entering Albuquerque along the modern version of Route 66.

Downtown Albuquerque

The old Route 66 is Central Avenue, still Albuquerque's main street. Three of the city's most interesting areas for visitors are along the historic highway, and, appropriately enough, you need a car to get between them or to do much else around town.

The short stretch of Central Avenue in the modern downtown is a quick walk from the convention center, the focal point of activities for many people staying in the city. The highlight of the neighborhood is the flamboyant KiMo Theater (423 Central Avenue Northwest, 505/764-1700), built in 1927 to house vaudeville acts. Native American motifs inspired the fanciful Art Deco facade and interior. Home now to special performing arts events, the KiMo is open daily for a free look when the stage is bare.

Just down the street, Cafe (216 Central Avenue Southwest, 505/242-8244), offers contemporary exhibitions, performances and events with an avant-garde edge. Also nearby, La Compania de Teatro de Albuquerque (518 1st Street, 505/242-7929), the state's largest bilingual theater, performs classic and modern plays in English and Spanish from fall through spring.

Much of the commerce downtown is oriented toward the area's workforce, though a smattering of shops around the convention center will interest visitors. Two spots worth seeking out are the Richard Levy Gallery (514 Central Avenue Southwest, 505/766-9888), for contemporary fine art, and The Cathedral Shop, with folk art from around the world, in St. John's Episcopal Cathedral (318 Silver Southwest, 505/247-1581). The downtown is on a human scale, unlike some skyscraper-dominated city centers, and many areas are pleasant to wander by day.

Old Town

Today's downtown grew up around the railroad depot, which the Atchison, Topeka, and Santa Fe deliberately built a couple of miles east of the original village, now known as Old Town. An area bounded by Central Avenue, Rio Grande Boulevard and Mountain Road, the neighborhood retains much of its architectural integrity and some vestiges of historic character.

Settled in the traditional Spanish style, Old Town features blocks of low adobe buildings surrounding a central plaza. The lovely San Felipe de Neri Church, dating to 1793, graces one side of the plaza, maintaining its dignity despite the trinket-shop atmosphere of some of the nearby streets. Named to honor King Philip V of Spain, the church initially had a simple facade that was altered in the late nineteenth century to include the distinctive twin spires, added to give an air of European refinement.

Old Town offers the only concentration of shops for easy browsing on foot within the city, and some of the stores are worth a serious look. Mariposa Gallery (113 Romero Northwest, 505/842-9097) exhibits top contemporary crafts, many from New Mexico artists. Just down the street, a few places excel with Native American artwork, particularly Tanner Chaney Gallery (410 Romero Northwest, 505/247-2242) and Adobe Gallery (413 Romero Northwest, 505/243-8485). You can also buy less expensive pieces of lower quality directly from Indians spreading their wares on blankets under a plaza portal.

Andy Gunderson's Rancho Viejo Antiques (2104 Charlevoix Northwest, 505/242-4191) sells Spanish colonial period furnishings, sometimes a great value. Another spot for regional bargains, Potpourri (121 Romero Northwest, 505/243-4087), can supply you with chiles and other necessities for cooking New Mexican meals back home.

The Albuquerque Museum (2000 Mountain Northwest, 505/243-7255), on the northwest edge of Old Town, presents rotating exhibitions of art, history and science, plus a long-term show on the city's development. The staff also provide regular free guided tours of Old Town. Closed Monday, the museum charges no admission.

Across the street and a short block east, two bronze dinosaurs welcome visitors to the Museum of Natural History (1801 Mountain Northwest, 505/841-8837). It houses changing exhibitions, but is best known for its volcano simulation and an "Evolator" ride which transports you back in time to the age of the dinosaurs. Open daily, the museum costs $4 for adults and $1 for children from 3 to 11.

The Indian Pueblo Cultural Center (2401 12th Street Northwest, 505/843-7270) is a short drive away, about a block north of Interstate 40. The museum portion of the facility is rather spare, although it is informative on an introductory level. The Center devotes most of its space to the sale of crafts of moderate price and quality. Open daily, IPCC charges $2.50 admission for adults and $1 for kids over 4.

The Rio Grande Zoo (903 10th Street Southwest, 505/843-7413) nestles between Old Town and downtown. An enticing park spread over 60 acres, it has an ambitious collection of animals in naturalistic settings, including an African savanna, a tropical rain forest, a primate island and a *lobo* (wolf) woods. Open daily, the zoo costs $4 for adults and $2 for the younger members of your party.

University of New Mexico Area

Also along Central Avenue, on the other side of downtown, the University of New Mexico dominates the neighborhood just east of Interstate 25. The campus is attractive and the nearby streets offer that combination of funk and fascination you often find around major colleges.

The main point of interest for us is the Tamarind Institute (108 Cornell Southeast, 505/277-3901). A printmaking studio as well as sales gallery, Tamarind has been a significant fixture on New Mexico's art scene since 1970. It may be the best place in the state to buy prints done by excellent artists—many of whom come to Tamarind for residencies—at reasonable prices. Tamarind is open during the day Monday through Friday and by appointment.

The university houses two fine art museums as well, the Jonson Gallery (1909 Las Lomas Northeast, 505/277-4967) and the University Art Museum (Central at Cornell, 505/277-4001). The former, in the home of the late modernist painter Raymond Jonson, shows his work, that of the Transcendentalist painting group, and contemporary art. The University Art Museum hosts changing exhibitions of nineteenth and twentieth century American and European art. Both are free and open Tuesday through Friday, and Tuesday night. The University Art Museum opens Sunday afternoons as well.

The Maxwell Museum of Anthropology (University and Grand Northeast, 505/277-4405) displays artifacts and folk art from its international collection, which has a special emphasis on the native cultures of the Southwest. Also free, it's open Monday through Saturday and Sunday afternoons.

The university helps support the performing arts in Albuquerque, too. Popejoy Hall, close to the Art Museum along Central, hosts the New Mexico Symphony and other local groups—including the New Mexico Ballet Company, Albuquerque Children's Theater and the Civic Light Opera—in addition to sponsoring touring shows from out of town. Call 505/277-3121 for information on concerts and other events.

Just east of the campus, near the intersection of Dartmouth and University, are a handful of galleries. From here the next few blocks of Central up to Nob Hill feature an eclectic mix of stores and boutiques. Nob Hill, at the corner of Carlisle, was one of the first shopping centers built west of the Mississippi. It seems tiny today for its purpose, but the revitalized Southwest Moderne facade is quaintly authentic.

The New Mexico Repertory Theater (228 Gold Southwest, 505/243-4500), the state's only resident professional company, has its headquarters near the university. The season runs from October to May, with performances both here and in Santa Fe.

The North Valley and Corrales

The Rio Grande flows lazily through Albuquerque's north valley and the neighboring village of Corrales, still pastoral enclaves in the modern city. The river continues to water a variety of nurseries and horse farms, and the area retains some of its old Spanish charm, particularly in parts of Corrales.

From Old Town, head north on Rio Grande Boulevard, skirting the river's east bank. After a few miles you reach the north valley's rural calm. There aren't many compelling places to stop, but we enjoy the Anderson Valley Vineyards (4920 Rio Grande Boulevard, 505/344-7266), a winery nestled under lofty cottonwoods. Tours and tastings are free.

On the west side of the Rio Grande, farther north, Corrales provides more diversions, including a few colorful shops and restaurants spread along the main street. The small, free Los Colores Museum (4499 Corrales Road, 505/898-5077) showcases weaving and textiles.

South of Corrales, off Unser Avenue Northwest, the Petroglyph National Monument offers the world's largest accessible collection of prehistoric rock art. More than 15,000 ancient images adorn an escarpment rimming five extinct volcanoes. The four trails that wind through the petroglyphs range from easy to challenging in terrain. The park is open daily for $1 per vehicle.

Special Annual Events

The largest hot-air ballooning event in the world, the Albuquerque International Balloon Fiesta, fills the skies of early October with a kaleidoscope of color. The organizers stage special activities daily but the major thrills for the general public are the mass ascensions of nearly seven hundred balloons that occur the first two Saturdays and Sundays of the month. A spectacular sight, they will dazzle even the most jaded of travelers. Plan to arrive before dawn and mingle on the launching site with the crews as they prepare to loft shortly after daylight. The event takes place at Balloon Fiesta Park on the city's far north side. Parking is $3 per car, with an admission of $2 for adults; kids under 12 are free. Call 505/821-1000 for more information.

Just a few weeks earlier, starting the weekend after Labor Day, the New Mexico State Fair is a genuine local tradition. It features everything from professional rodeos, horseracing and heifer contests to a 40-acre midway, Indian and Spanish "villages" and a trove of junk food. Like similar events elsewhere, it's as corny as it is fun. The State Fair grounds are in the heart of the city just off Central Avenue (300 San Pedro Northeast, 800/253-3247 or 505/265-1791). Parking costs $4 per car and admission is $1–2 a person.

The Fiery Foods Show isn't as grand as the State Fair or the Balloon Fiesta, but the "Hottest Show on Earth" does spice up life in early February. Vendors of chile products and other zesty foods come from around the world to introduce their goods to retailers and restaurateurs. A portion of the Convention Center event is open to the public at a nominal admission for tastings, food demonstrations and discussions. You can try and buy hundreds of treats ranging from salsas and sauces to chile-laced chocolate and peanut brittle. For more information, contact Sunbelt Shows, 505/873-2187.

Lodging

Albuquerque accommodations on the whole are typical of cities across the country, a mix of high-rise hotels and sprawling motels, both dully standardized. We mention the best of these options along with a selection of smaller and more charming spots. Rates stay about the same year-round except for moderate increases during the State Fair and the Balloon Fiesta, and substantial reductions on weekends at places oriented to business travelers.

Easily the most distinctive of the big hotels is the downtown La Posada de Albuquerque (125 Second Street Northwest, 800/777-5732 or 505/242-9090). Conrad Hilton built it in 1939 as his second hotel and the first in his home state. On the National Register of Historic Places, the beautifully refurbished property retains its old character with fresh elegance. Rates run from $72 to $102.

The fanciest of the hotels in the heart of the business district, and the newest, is the twin-peaked Hyatt Regency Albuquerque (330 Tijeras, 800/233-1234 or 505/842-

1234), where rates average about $120. The Albuquerque Doubletree (201 Marquette Street Northwest, 800/528-0444 or 505/247-3344) at $108 is a short step down in price as well as class. East of downtown, the Albuquerque Marriott (2101 Louisiana Northeast, 800/228-9290 or 505/881-6800), starting at $126, won't disappoint if you're looking for upscale comforts. The Holiday Inn Pyramid (5151 San Francisco Northeast, 800/544-0623 or 505/821-3333), just off Interstate 25 on the north side of the city, offers more sophistication than many of its roadside cousins at rates beginning at $96. All four hotels cater primarily to business travelers.

There are a number of airport hotels. The closest to the terminals is the AMFAC (2910 Yale, 800/227-1117 or 505/843-7000), where rates start at $82. The Best Western Airport Inn (2400 Yale, 800/528-1234 or 505/242-7022) is not much farther and offers better value at about $25 less.

A top choice for small, quaint and friendly is the Corrales Inn (505/897-4422), in the neighboring village where much of the metropolitan area's remaining allure is concentrated. The moderately priced ($65) B&B has six rooms that open into a fountain-splashed courtyard with a hot tub. Half the quarters share the contemporary Southwestern style of the exterior, and the other three feature Victorian, Oriental and hot-air–balloon decor.

Casita Chamisa (850 Chamisal, 505/897-4644), in a rural area of the north valley, sits over the site of an archaeological dig. At breakfast you can watch a video of the excavation of the property's Pueblo ruins. The B&B offers an indoor lap pool for swimmers and two units, one of which holds a family of up to six. Rates begin at $85.

Within walking distance of Old Town, Casa de Sueños (310 Rio Grande Southwest, 505/247-4560) borders the Albuquerque Country Club golf course. Once an artist's studio, the intimate adobe compound surrounds a peaceful garden. Back downtown, the W.E. Mauger Estate (701 Roma Northwest, 505/242-8755) is one of the last remnants of Victorian Albuquerque. The restored turn-of-the-century home, with six accommodations, welcomes guests elegantly for $70 to $90. Both B&Bs, like the others recommended, provide private baths.

For personality at a pittance, try one of the original Route 66 motor courts. Among the possibilities, the Monterey Motel (2402 Central Avenue Southwest, 505/243-3554) has the nicest rooms—however modest—and a pool. Built in 1932, it holds the distinction of being the oldest AAA-rated motel on Route 66. El Vado (2500 Central Avenue Southwest, 505/243-4594) is marked by a neon sign you won't miss and a vintage exterior, designed by the same architect as Santa Fe's beautiful El Rey Motel. De Anza (4301 Central Avenue Northeast, 505/255-1654) offers less in funky charm but it's worth the cost, especially if you're looking for a bargain close to the university or the State Fair. All three places charge around $30.

Restaurants

While Santa Fe boasts a number of upscale restaurants that think of themselves as up-to-date in all ways, Albuquerque specializes in hearty cooking and value pricing. Even the most polished establishments are less pretentious and pricy than their counterparts to the north.

The two most sophisticated restaurants are within a few blocks of each other on Central Avenue, in the neighborhood just east of the University of New Mexico. The Monte Vista Fire Station (3201 Central Avenue Northeast, 505/255-2424) features contemporary American dishes with Southwestern accents. The kitchen takes care in the selection of ingredients and in the preparations, seasoning with subtlety. The changing menu always includes a wide range of fresh fish and seafood selections.

The fare is equally imaginative and a little more robust at Scalo (3500 Central Avenue Northeast in the Nob Hill Shopping Center, 505/255-8782). The kitchen knows its northern Italian dishes intimately, and presents them with a flair that matches the urbane sparkle of the dining room.

Another option for cosmopolitan cooking, closer to downtown, is the Artichoke Cafe (424 Central Avenue Southeast, 505/243-0200), where the selections are always satisfying and sometimes superb. Prairie Star (Jemez Dam Road off Highway 44, Bernalillo, 505/867-3327) offers contemporary Southwestern fare at dinner only and provides sweeping views of the Sandias as a bonus. Reservations are usually necessary at all of the aforementioned restaurants.

Notable New Mexican food is scattered throughout the city. On the fringes of downtown, M&J's Sanitary Tortilla Factory (403 Second Street, 505/242-4890) serves some of the best local cooking in the state from lunch until early evening. Try the House Special, *carne adovada* enchiladas made with blue corn tortillas, or the daily special. The simple and cheap cafe is just a few blocks off Interstate 25, making it an ideal stop between Santa Fe and the Albuquerque airport.

Like M&J's, Duran Central Pharmacy (1815 Central Avenue Northwest, 505/247-4141) has a devoted local clientele for its New Mexican specialties, offered here with old-fashioned lunch-counter atmosphere. It's an easy walk or drive from Old Town. Near the university, El Patio (142 Harvard Southeast, 505/268-4245) serves big, flavorful combination plates, as does Sadie's (6230 Fourth Northwest, 505/345-5339) in the north valley. For more charm, check out the patio at El Pinto (10500 Fourth Northwest, 505/898-1771), in the north valley, or the rambling old hacienda that houses Rancho de Corrales (505/897-3131).

Albuquerque has some excellent, moderately priced Asian restaurants, usually open for lunch and dinner and quite pleasant despite some inauspicious locations and buildings. India Kitchen (6910 Montgomery Northeast, 505/884-2333) is off the beaten path for visitors, but worth a detour for good, spicy cooking. Ajay Gupta gave up an engineering career to introduce Albuquerque to the delightful tastes of his native Indian food. Ask his advice on what to order and tell him how hot you want it. The restaurant is in a shopping strip near Louisiana Boulevard, one of the city's main streets.

Bangkok Cafe and Malaysian Bay Oriental Seafood are other good choices for Asian cooking. Malaysian Bay (1826 Eubank Northeast, 505/293-5597) is in the same quadrant of Albuquerque as India Kitchen. The Taiwanese owner and chefs turn out inventive fish and seafood, mostly Chinese in inspiration, fragrant with soy, ginger, oyster sauce. Try the chile-charged sesame dumplings for openers. Bangkok Cafe (5901 Central Avenue Northeast, 505/255-5036) always fills our need for a fix of Thai food. While the kitchen can prepare many of the dishes with mild seasoning for tender palates, the staff is also happy to tingle your tongue with zesty, piquant flavoring.

Fans of down-home American fare have good options as well, a variety of places that are inexpensive to moderate in price, open for lunch and dinner, and suitable for family meals. The 66 Diner (1405 Central Avenue Northeast, 505/247-1421) and a chain restaurant, the Black-Eyed Pea (601 Juan Tabo Northeast at Interstate 40, 505/299-0997), serve heaping plates of country favorites such as chicken-fried steak, meat loaf, fried catfish and mashed potatoes. At the Pea, don't miss the broccoli-rice casserole.

Barbecue is the specialty at Powdrell's three restaurants. We usually choose the one at 11309 Central Avenue Northeast (505/298-6766), near the eastern edge of the city, not far from the Black-Eyed Pea. The Quarters (905 Yale, 505/843-7505) also makes good barbecue—the smoked turkey is particularly tasty. It's a popular bar too.

The barn-like Frontier (2400 Central Avenue Southeast across from the university, 505/266-0550) is an amazing spot. The cheap food is full of flavor, and fun to eat in a setting that mixes orange Naugahyde, wagon-wheel chandeliers, and paintings of "Duke" Wayne. The Frontier attracts an eccentric but interesting crowd of students and savvy eaters looking for a bargain burger, burrito or butter-laden cinnamon roll. Just staying open 24 hours sets the Frontier apart from almost every other spot in town, and makes it convenient if you've arrived hungrry at the nearby airport at an odd hour.

We sometimes stop at the Frontier for breakfast, but the nearby Double Rainbow (3416 Central Avenue Southeast, 505/255-6633) entices us too. The coffee, in multiple forms, is topnotch, as are the sophisticated baked goods. Grandma's (141 Osuna Northwest, 505/345-1283) takes you back home for breakfast, with robust American and Southwestern dishes that will keep you going all day.

Chapter Ten
◆◆◆◆◆◆◆◆◆◆◆

Mountain Adventures

THE MOUNTAIN scenery around Santa Fe is some of the grandest in the Rockies. The peaks are higher in Colorado, the canyons are more colorful in Arizona, the wilderness area is larger in Idaho, the hot springs are more torrid in Wyoming and the sky is bigger in Montana, but northern New Mexico is one of the few places in the Rocky Mountains where all of these natural features exist together. The total effect is stunning, for hiking, climbing, biking, skiing, camping, trail riding, fishing, river rafting or just taking a short drive from Santa Fe.

Seeing the best of the mountain scenery requires some exertion and preparation. Parts of the areas described here can be viewed from a car, as in the case of the high road to Taos, but much more can be experienced on foot—hiking, climbing or skiing.

Hiking can be enjoyed most of the year, except after heavy snows. In any season hikers have to be prepared for extreme changes in weather. Storms can move in very quickly, especially on summer afternoons. Almost every year people get lost or trapped in a storm and never return. Hiking boots, warm clothing, water and topographical maps are useful even for short walks and are essential for longer ones. The local chapter of the Sierra Club has published a helpful guide, *Day Hikes in the Santa Fe Area* (1986), available in local bookstores. *A Hikers and Climbers Guide to the Sandias*, by Mike Hill (University of New Mexico Press, 2nd edition, 1983) provides similar advice for the Albuquerque mountains.

Northern New Mexico is popular for both downhill and cross-country skiing in the winter. The snow is usually deep and often powdery from December until Easter, and the sun is more intense than anywhere else in the Rockies. The Santa Fe Ski Area is the closest downhill center, thirty to forty-five minutes up a good road from the city. The Taos Ski Valley, about two hours away, is larger and has more exciting runs for advanced skiers (see Chapter 8). Sandia Crest Ski Area, adjacent to Albuquerque, is smaller than the others and attracts mostly locals and less-experienced skiers. These facilities, and several others nearby, provide high-altitude skiing, starting around 10,000 feet, with panoramic views of the mountains.

Opportunities for cross-country skiing are abundant. Some cross-country trails are mentioned below, but many more are described by Jim Burns and Cheryl Lemanski in *Skiing the Sun: Ski Touring in New Mexico's National Forests* (Los Alamos Ski Touring, 1985). There are a variety of places to rent equipment in Santa Fe, Taos and Albuquerque.

Horseback riding is a less strenuous means of mountain sightseeing. Both of the Tesuque resorts, Rancho Encantado and the Bishop's Lodge, allow non-guests on trail rides when extra horses are available, though the chances of getting a mount are better at Camel Rock Stables north of Santa Fe (505/986-0408). The trail rides stay at fairly low altitudes and don't allow much independent exploration, but the physical burden at least is shifted upward from the feet to the better-padded parts of the body.

Mountain bikes are another option. Numerous area dealers rent them. Get a copy of the *New Mexico Bicyclists Guide*, compiled by the Highway Department, at almost any of the rental shops.

Camping and fishing sites are scattered throughout the Santa Fe National Forest, which surrounds the city on three sides with a million and a half acres of mountain streams and lakes, backpacking opportunities and campgrounds. The Carson National Forest outside of Taos offers similar largess. The Forest Service sells an inexpensive map that shows all the possibilities, and can provide current information at 505/988-6940. For fishing licenses, contact the New Mexico Game and Fish Department at 505/827-7880.

Reliable outfitters for fishing gear and guides are High Desert Angler (435 S. Guadalupe, 505/988-7688) in Santa Fe and Los Rios Anglers (226-B N. Pueblo, 505/758-2798) in Taos. For hiking, climbing and camping gear, check with Santa Fe's Base Camp (121 W. San Francisco, 505/982-9707), Taos Mountain Outfitters (114 S. Plaza, 505/758-9292), or Albuquerque's Sandia Mountain Outfitters (1700 Juan Tabo, 505/293-9725).

Among all the places to enjoy the surrounding mountains, we focus here on a few of our favorites. The chances are strong that at least one of the options will fit any needs you have for high adventure.

Hyde Memorial Park and the Santa Fe Ski Area

The mountain access closest to Santa Fe is along 17-mile Hyde Park Road, which ends at the Santa Fe Ski Area. The road climbs from 7,000 feet in town to 10,260 feet at the top, passing through a national forest and a state park. The views are wonderful from the road, particularly when the aspen are turning in the fall, but they only hint at what can be seen on the many foot trails nearby.

Several of the trails are relatively easy, short and well-marked. The Chamisa Trail starts five and a half miles from the beginning of the road, at the Forest Service sign indicating Trail 183. It climbs 700 feet through juniper, pine and fir forests to a crest one and a quarter miles from the trailhead—a good spot for a picnic. Hikers can stop at the crest and return from there to the car, or can continue on the path downhill for another mile to a grassy meadow and the Big Tesuque Creek.

The Hyde Park Circle is a longer walk, about five miles, but no more strenuous. It begins at Hyde Park headquarters, directly across the road from the small general store. The trail, marked by three blazes (notches cut on trees), climbs steeply at first and then levels off gradually along a ridge. At the top are picnic tables and a magnificent 360-degree view. Two paths lead back to the main road down the other side of the ridge. Just beyond the picnic tables is a branch of the trail jutting off to the right, a shorter but less scenic way down. The main trail continues straight at the junction. Both paths end at Hyde Park Road about a mile north of the park store.

Farther up the road are a number of longer and more difficult trails, two of which are excellent for cross-country skiing in the winter. One of the most beautiful at any time of the year follows the Aspen Vista Road to Tesuque Peak. The path starts at the Aspen Vista Picnic Area, a few miles below the ski basin. The first two and a half miles are through an aspen forest, gorgeous in the fall and wonderful for skiing in the winter. After crossing four forks of the Tesuque Creek, the trail heads up Tesuque Peak for three and a half miles through fir and spruce, affording fine views along the way of the Rio Grande Valley and Santa Fe. Even in midsummer you are likely to find snow on the upper part of the trail before reaching the 12,040-foot summit.

The Winsor Trail is also good for both hiking and cross-country skiing. The trailhead is on the north side of the lower parking lot of the ski area. The trail climbs abruptly at first through aspen and spruce for about half a mile. At the top is a meadow and a boundary fence for the Pecos Wilderness. From there the trail slopes gently downhill for about one and a half miles to the Rio Nambe. From this point you might follow the creek to the right about a mile and a half to Nambe Lake, although there is not a maintained trail in this direction. Most hikers stay on Winsor Trail to Puerto Nambe, another mile uphill. The ascent is steep, but it offers grand views of Santa Fe Baldy, Lake Peak and Penitente Peak. From the meadow at Puerto Nambe the Winsor Trail goes on to Spirit Lake, another two miles, and ultimately ends up near Cowles, on the other side of the range. Sky Line Trail goes off from Puerto Nambe to Lake Katherine and the summit of Santa Fe Baldy, three miles away.

Pecos Wilderness

The Pecos Wilderness can be entered by the Winsor Trail from the ski area, but the most common approach is from Route 63. The highway starts about twenty miles east of Santa Fe, near the Pecos National Monument, a pueblo abandoned in the 1830s. A paved road follows the Pecos River north for 13 miles to the village of Tererro. Six miles farther on graded dirt is a junction where the town of Cowles used to be. Nearby are several national forest campgrounds that provide access to the wilderness.

Most of the marked trails in the area are strenuous and require a long day to enjoy fully. It's best to camp overnight or start very early in the morning from Santa Fe.

One of the most scenic trails goes to Pecos Baldy Lake and Peak. It starts at Jack's Creek Campground, three miles north of Cowles. It climbs steadily at first for a thousand feet over two and a half miles. In a grassy meadow at that point, with beautiful distant views, the trail forks left. Over the next two miles the trail, marked occasionally by posts, goes through an aspen grove, another meadow and a pine forest, and then drops down to Jack's Creek. From the creek there is a steep two-mile ascent through pines to the timber line and Pecos Baldy Lake. The summit of Pecos Baldy is 1,100 feet directly above the lake, another mile of hiking along the path through Horsethief Meadow.

✕ Bandelier National Monument

Bandelier is one of the most fascinating places in the Santa Fe region. The site of ancient Pueblo settlements, abandoned before the founding of Santa Fe, the park contains cliff dwellings, excavated and unexcavated ruins, sacred places, waterfalls, a small museum, complete camping facilities, a wilderness area for backpacking and superb hiking trails. The areas most developed for sight-seeing can be enjoyed on a half-day trip from Santa Fe, but there is enough of interest in the monument to fill a week.

The 40-mile drive from Santa Fe is beautiful, particularly after leaving U.S. 84/285 and going west toward the Jemez Mountains on Route 502/4. Near the Rio Grande the road passes less than a mile from San Ildefonso Pueblo, always worth a detour, and then climbs the Pajarito Plateau. From the high spots on the plateau there are grand views eastward to the Sangre de Cristo Mountains before the road descends into Frijoles Canyon and to the park headquarters.

The primary ruins and cliff dwellings can be seen on a

short walk from the visitors' center, though serious hikers have lots of other options. A backcountry trail map, as well as a guidebook about the trails, is available at the visitors' center. One of the best day hikes, covering 13 miles, goes to the Stone Lions Shrine, an ancient ceremonial carving still sacred to the Pueblos and likely to be ringed with deer antler offerings. The hike is difficult at one point, but it includes fine views of Frijoles Canyon from above, a range of vegetation, an unexcavated ruin and mountain panoramas.

Bandelier is open year-round, but fluctuations in the federal budget can affect some services. For current information on hours and facilities call 505/672-3861.

The nearby Puye Cliff Dwellings, off Highway 30, offer a similar ancient setting that's far less crowded and developed. You may have to make some of your own trails, but the forlorn mesa exerts a powerful spell that's likely to linger a lifetime.

Other Areas

There are numerous other interesting spots farther from Santa Fe in the mountains of northern New Mexico. North of the city on U.S. 84 are Ghost Ranch and the fabulous vistas painted there by Georgia O'Keeffe. Farther along the same highway are the towns of Tierra Amarilla, close to two recreational lakes, and Chama, originating point for narrow-gauge rail trips on the Cumbres and Toltec Scenic Railroad.

Wheeler Peak, the highest point in New Mexico at 13,161 feet, is north of Taos, as is the beautiful drive to the Taos Ski Valley. The Rio Grande Gorge, a deep canyon that illustrates how *grande* the river was before dams, is closer to the town. The Rio Grande State Park is a good place to explore the canyon or fish the river, though the views are more dramatic from the bridge on U.S. 64.

Whitewater rafting on this stretch of the river is thrilling in the early summer and just languorously scenic by the end of the season. Two rafting companies with toll-free numbers are Rio Grande River Tours (800/525-4966, 505/758-0762) and Southwest Wilderness Center (800/ 869-7238, 505/983-7262).

The region around Mora is not known well even in New Mexico. Settled by French trappers in the early nineteenth century, the tiny villages nearby have not changed much since then. In the late summer and early fall, plan a stop near La Cueva at the Salmon Ranch Raspberry Farm for fruit and jam. There is a splendid mountain drive from Mora through Guadalupita to Black Lake and the Angel Fire Ski Basin, not shown on many maps.

West of Santa Fe, Route 4 passes through scenic sections of the Jemez Mountains. There is not much to see in Los Alamos, where the atomic bomb was developed, but farther along the road is the Valle Grande, an enormous caldera, or collapsed volcano. A partially unpaved intersecting road, Route 126, crosses high country to Cuba, near the southern boundary of the Jicarilla Apache Reservation. Route 4 continues through Jemez Springs, with its roadside hot springs, and connects with Route 44, passing close to the Jemez, Zia and Santa Ana pueblos. Since Route 44 leads to Bernalillo, just north of Albuquerque, this can be a long but interesting way to reach Albuquerque from Santa Fe.

Chapter Eleven
♦♦♦♦♦♦♦♦♦♦♦♦

Music, Markets and More

EVERY summer Santa Fe becomes an international arts center, offering a variety and quality of arts events that rival any American city during the same months. From the opening of the opera in early July through Indian Market in late August, a flurry of gallery openings, special shows, concerts and other performances dominate social and economic life. More relaxed and secluded the rest of the year, closer to its historical character, Santa Fe in the summer becomes a little bloated with sophistication, both genuine and phony. But it also reaches a peak of artistry that is a natural culmination of its remarkable cultural heritage.

Many Santa Feans actually prefer the secret arts season of the spring, fall and winter. The talents are seldom as renowned, but the performing arts still flourish and the local atmosphere is more conducive to appreciation. If you want culture without the crowds, skip to the end of the chapter for tips.

The Santa Fe Opera

When John Crosby founded the Santa Fe Opera in 1957, opera in the United States was dominated by European talent and repetitive stagings of standard repertory. Crosby was convinced that opera could be more exciting, innovative and American. He planned carefully for several years to create an outdoor summer festival that would feature and cultivate American musical talent. He chose Santa Fe for a location because most larger cities "have a great deal of rain, lots of mosquitos and lots of airplanes overhead."

The original opera house was acoustically sound but not very grand, built at a cost of $115,000 to provide seating, on wooden benches, for 480 patrons. It burned during the eleventh season and was replaced by opening night of the next year, after a Gargantuan effort, with a magnificent new theater that can hold almost 1,400 people comfortably. Situated in a large natural bowl in the Tesuque hills, just north of Santa Fe, the theater is open on the sides, and partially open on the top to the resplendent evening skies. Even people who prefer other kinds of music attend the opera for its setting.

The productions are lavish and adventuresome, requiring a company of nearly 500 professionals as singers, orchestra players, technicians, designers and administrators. The emphasis is on new and neglected works. The annual season customarily includes some standard repertory, but the old warhorses are usually less exciting for the performers and the audience than the seldom-seen works. The Santa Fe Opera, despite its relative youth among major American companies, holds the national record for premieres, averaging one a summer.

The season opens in early July and runs until the end of August. In July performances are on Wednesdays, Fridays and Saturdays; in August they are daily. Though admission is a bargain compared to opera prices in most cities, it is not cheap. For people on a tight budget, standing room is an incredible value, costing about the same as most movies. For additional information call 505/982-3851. The box office number is 505/982-3855.

Santa Fe Chamber Music Festival

Many people who have never attended the Chamber Music Festival have an indelible image of the event from the stunning posters donated for many years by Georgia O'Keeffe, one of the festival's most devoted fans during her lifetime. The music invariably lives up to the promise of the posters, spiritually powerful, immediate and complex. Though the festival is fifteen years younger than the opera, it has nearly the same level of national and international recognition.

As in the case of the opera, the setting for performances is delightful. Festival concerts are in the Museum of Fine Arts' St. Francis Auditorium, an intimate hall modeled on a Spanish mission chapel. A roster of some forty stellar artists from around the world fills the auditorium almost daily during the seven-week season for concerts, discussions and public rehearsals.

Each year the festival features an American composer and an American quartet in residence. The composer creates a commissioned piece for the festival, directs rehearsals of the work and explains aspects of its composition during discussion rehearsals. The quartet performs as a group and in larger ensembles.

Since 1987 the Festival has celebrated the folkloric musical traditions of Latin America through its Music of the Americas series. Concerts by musicians who have usually not performed before in the U.S. are complemented with lecture-demonstrations.

The festival season opens in early July and closes near

the end of August. Concerts are held most evenings, and there are other events daily. Call 505/983-2075 for the specifics.

Santa Fe Desert Chorale

The Santa Fe Desert Chorale is a youngster compared to the Opera and Chamber Music Festival, but its aspirations are equally lofty. Lawrence Bandfield directs professional singers from throughout the country in an ambitious and innovative program of choral music from the Renaissance to the avant-garde. Performances in a variety of languages are staged primarily at the Santuario de Guadalupe during June and July, and take place periodically in Albuquerque as well. Call 505/988-7505 for the repertory and reservations.

Maria Benitez Dance Company

The premier flamenco dancer in America, Maria Benitez grew up in Taos and maintains a home in Santa Fe. Most of the year she and her troupe are on tour, but they return to Santa Fe each summer for a season of energetic, passionate and popular performances. Benitez leaves no one bored or distracted.

In recent years she has been performing at the Picacho Plaza Hotel, though the venue has shifted from time to time in the past. For performance information call the hotel at 505/982-5591 or check the local newspaper for ads.

Southwest Repertory Theater

A fixture on the summer theatre scene since the late 1980s, the Southwest Repertory Theater presents high-quality classics from mid-July through mid-August. Generally the semiprofessional company offers one musical and two plays in repertory at the James A. Little Theater on the campus of the New Mexico School for the Deaf. Call 505/ 982-1336 for performance information or reservations.

Gallery Openings

The opening of a new show in a gallery can be as much of a performance as anything produced by the opera. The artist is center stage, obligingly or not playing a complex variety of roles as interpreter of the work, loyal servant of the gallery and friend of patrons. The fun starts for observers when other performers from the gallery and the crowd compete for the same roles and the spotlight. Never the best time to see an artist's new work, openings are nonetheless lively events and among the best entertainment values in town.

While they occur during the entire year, openings are far more concentrated in the summer than at any other time. Check for listings in the Friday "Pasatiempo" section of the *New Mexican*, the local newspaper, or call favorite galleries. Admission is always free, and usually the wine is, too.

Indian Market

Indian Market, on the third weekend of August, is always Santa Fe's busiest time. Over four hundred of the best Indian artists in the country, chosen carefully each year to maintain high standards of quality, display and sell their finest work on the plaza. The assembled trove of traditional and contemporary art attracts a swarm of collectors, dealers and the curious. The professionals among them show up on the plaza as early as 5:00 A.M. on Saturday to beat each other to the best of the pottery, jewelry, weaving and other work. The most frenzied round of buying is over before the sun is fully visible on the horizon, but the selection remains excellent, and the crowds remain huge, for the rest of the weekend. Prices, as high as the quality, can shock the uninitiated.

The sponsor of the event is the Southwestern Association on Indian Affairs (505/983-5220). The organization was formed in 1922 to defeat the Bursum Bill, legislation that would have taken land and water rights from the Pueblos, but its primary purpose today is the preservation and encouragement of Southwestern Indian art.

Spanish Market

Spanish Market is not as popular or well-known as Indian Market, but is the best occasion in the United States to see and buy traditional Spanish colonial crafts and their contemporary offshoots. The Spanish Colonial Arts Society sponsors the annual fair, held the last full weekend of July, to recognize artistic achievement in local crafts. Juries of experts give monetary awards in the areas of woodcarving, ironwork, weaving, *colcha* stitchery, jewelry, furniture and straw inlay. The work is often stunning and always an impressive display of the persistence of the Santa Fe heritage. Few of the items you'll see are routinely available in Santa Fe shops or galleries. This is the place to buy them, at prices quite reasonable for the craftsmanship involved. Traditional crafts are displayed around the sides of the plaza and the contemporary work is along Lincoln Avenue. Contact the Spanish Colonial Arts Society at 505/983-4038 for more information.

The Secret Arts Season

After the Opera and Chamber Music Festival wrap up in August, and their musicians scatter to the ends of the globe, local performing artists and companies have the stage to themselves through the next spring. They don't have the resources and international stature of the summer institutions, but they don't lack talent and commitment.

The New Mexico Repertory Theater, performing from October to April, has established a solid regional reputation for its adventuresome productions. The company handles the classics capably, but puts its most earnest energy into contemporary plays by writers such as Sam Shepard, David Mamet, Tom Stoppard, Milcha Sanchez-Scott and New Mexico's own Mark Medoff.

The Rep performs at the almost venerable Armory for the Arts, 1050 Old Pecos Trail. The building was a deteriorating national guard armory until a group of artists adopted it as a home during the 1970s and transformed it gradually into a superb small theatre. Call 505/984-2226 for performance information and reservations.

Student productions at the College of Santa Fe during the school year are often high-caliber and they are performed in a fine facility, the campus's Greer Garson Theater (505/473-6511). Several less-established theatre groups are active in Santa Fe at various times of the year. The Santa Fe Actor's Theater (505/982-3581) works out of a converted railroad warehouse at 430 West Manhattan. The Railyard Performance Center (505/982-8309) also provides a stage for other events, often experimental in nature. The Santa Fe Community Theater (505/982-4262) operates around the calendar out of a fraying facility in a historic neighborhood at 142 East De Vargas. It stages the annual Fiesta Melodrama each September, lampooning the political and the pompous.

Santa Fe's two symphony orchestras perform from the fall through the spring. Both can fill an evening with luscious sound. The Orchestra of Santa Fe (505/988-4640), under the long-established direction of William Kirschke, presents a dozen or more concerts a season at the downtown Lensic Theater, 211 West San Francisco. The Mozart Festival in early February is particularly popular. The Orchestra's chamber music group, the Ensemble of Santa Fe, performs in the intimate, lovely Loretto Chapel. The Ensemble can be reached at 505/984-2501.

The Santa Fe Symphony (505/983-3530) was created by musicians who left the Orchestra in a dispute. Directed by Stewart Robertson, it has been growing steadily in stature since 1984. The Symphony uses the Sweeney Center, downtown at Marcy Street and Grant, for its concerts.

The sponsors of Spanish Market, the Spanish Colonial Arts Society (505/983-4038), started a Winter Market a few years ago, scheduled for the first full weekend in December. All artists and craftspeople juried into the summer show can participate in the lesser-known winter event, which attracts a smaller number of entrants. A great spot for Christmas shopping, the show is held usually at La Fonda Hotel on the plaza. The sponsors of Indian Market also hold a second event during the year. The Southwestern Association on Indian Affairs organizes the Santa Fe Powwow on Memorial Day weekend on Pojoaque Pueblo land north of Santa Fe some dozen miles. It features an Indian crafts market, dances and food booths.

Most literary activities in Santa Fe happen in the "off season." Writers were an important part of the original art colony and many live in the area today, including John Nichols, Scott Momaday, Tony Hillerman, Frank Waters and Elizabeth Tallent. Readings and workshops are presented on an occasional basis at the College of Santa Fe, the main public library and a number of bookstores, including the Bookroom (616 Canyon Road, 505/988-5323), Caxton's (216 W. San Francisco, 505/982-8911), Collected Works (208-B W. San Francisco, 505/988-4226), Garcia Street Books (376 Garcia at Acequia Madre, 505/986-0151) and Old Santa Fe Trail Bookstore and Coffee House (613 Old Santa Fe Trail, 505/988-8878). Recursos de Santa Fe (505/982-9301), which offers a fascinating range of educational programs, holds an annual writers' conference in early August that attracts a number of respected authors.

Chapter Twelve
◆◆◆◆◆◆◆◆◆◆◆◆◆

Fiestas and Traditional Ceremonies

ALL OF the Indian pueblos and many of the Spanish towns of New Mexico hold annual fiestas to celebrate their existence as communities. The fiestas are similar in some ways to annual festivities of other towns in the country—the Oktoberfests, county fairs, founder's day events and other occasions that reaffirm a local heritage. New Mexican fiestas are different, however, in one critical respect. They revolve around unique ceremonies that would be unimaginable in other parts of the country.

None of the fiestas are touted as tourist attractions or even publicized much outside the community. They are held primarily for residents and friends. Visitors are welcome, though, and may find a fiesta or other traditional ceremonial event the most fascinating time to be in the Santa Fe area.

Fiesta de Santa Fe

The Santa Fe Fiesta comes at the end of the crowded summer season, the weekend after Labor Day. Though a lot of tourists are still in the city through Christmas, the event coincides with an important turning point in the annual tourism cycle, the return of the city to its residents. For nine months or so after Fiesta each year locals will be able to find parking space downtown, obtain dinner reservations, sit peacefully on the plaza and otherwise enjoy where they live. Santa Fe becomes itself again during Fiesta, and in the process releases a bit of pent-up tension and creative craziness.

This was not Fiesta's original purpose, though it's not altogether inconsistent with the founding intent. Fiesta was started in 1712 to celebrate the Spanish reconquest of Santa Fe from the Pueblos in 1692–93. Many of the activities still focus on the city's seventeenth-century struggles, but others are more contemporary in origin and character.

Fiesta's first major event, the burning of Zozobra on Friday evening, is one of the twentieth-century embellishments. Zozobra, representing Old Man Gloom, is a 40-foot marionette, taller than almost any building in town. Will Shuster, one of the founders of the local art colony, created the creature in the 1920s. Initially Shuster and his friends burned a small Zozobra at an annual party in his backyard, to dispel gloom from the city in preparation for the rest of Fiesta. Long ago the event was moved to a city park, and now virtually everyone in town participates. While Zozobra flails his arms and groans miserably, the assembled citizenry torch the giant effigy in a fireworks ceremony more dramatic than any Fourth of July celebration.

Free of gloom for the next year, the crowd walks to the plaza, about a mile away, shouting "*Viva la Fiesta!*" Music, merriment, eating and parading continue on the plaza for the next two days.

On Saturday morning there is a children's pet parade. Almost every child in the city shows up in costume with a real or imaginary animal friend. It's so much fun that childless adults try to borrow kids for the day to accompany them in the parade.

In the afternoon specially selected and carefully rehearsed residents, on horseback in seventeenth-century dress, reenact Don Diego de Vargas's triumphant entry into the city in 1692. Being chosen to play the Don's role is a greater honor locally than being elected mayor. A grand ball in the evening ends the day's festivities, just as it did a couple of hundred years ago.

The big event during the day on Sunday is the Hysterical/Historical Parade, which is more of the former than the latter. Various neighborhood and civic groups compete to mount the most imaginative float, many of which comment caustically on local and national political issues. Fiesta concludes solemnly on Sunday night with mass in the cathedral and a candlelight procession from there to the Cross of the Martyrs, a hilltop memorial to the 23 Franciscan priests killed in the 1680 Pueblo Revolt.

Pueblo Fiestas

Every New Mexican pueblo holds an annual fiesta—also called a Feast Day—to commemorate its patron saint. Since each community, with the exception of one pair of communities, has a different patron saint, the celebrations are spread over the year. The majority happen to occur between June and September, during the busy tourism season, but they are definitely not intended as tourist attractions. Visitors are allowed as observers as long as they respect the religious rites and strictly adhere to local laws, which prohibit drinking, approaching or getting very close to a kiva, parking in an unauthorized area and (in most cases) photographing, sketching or recording any of the activities. A sign in one of the pueblos would apply to all:

We welcome you. We have always been friendly to visitors who appreciate that they are guests in our villages and respect our privacy. You will attend one of our ancient religious ceremonies. This ceremonial is as sacred to us as your church services are to you. We ask only that you always keep in mind the sacred nature of this ceremonial dance and be guided by the rules of our village government.

Events vary in significant ways among the different pueblos, but most fiestas have a common pattern. The day opens with a mass sometime between seven and ten in the morning. From the church there is a procession around the village plaza, which concludes when an image of the patron saint is placed in a bower, or shrine, in the plaza. Native dances start soon afterward and continue off and on until the late afternoon, when another procession returns the *santo* to the church.

The dances are usually the highlight of the day for residents and visitors alike. They bear no resemblance in form or purpose to what most Americans regard as dancing. They are prayers in motion, a demonstration of reverence for and harmony with the spiritual forces that pervade the world. The dances are highly repetitive, almost hypnotically monotonous to observers. Drums and a chorus provide a pulsing rhythm that changes in tempo and sometimes pauses unexpectedly. Most of the dances involve dozens or even hundreds of people. The dancers are dressed in clothing traditional for the particular dance, which can vary from breechcloths to full animal costumes. Usually dancers wear headdresses and the men's bodies are painted.

Different pueblos feature different dances for fiesta, and some of them change dances from year to year. The Corn Dance is the most common. Its presentation at Santo Domingo on August 4, when some five hundred residents participate, is particularly popular with tourists. The most unusual and striking of the fiesta dances is at San Ildefonso on January 23. The village's Buffalo Dance begins the evening before, lighted by log bonfires, and resumes at dawn with animal dancers descending from nearby hills, guided by the Game Priest dancer, who spreads sacred corn-meal to form a path. As the Corn Dance pays homage to what has been the main staple of the Pueblo diet for the past four thousand years, the Buffalo Dance expresses unity with the game hunted for meat over the same millenniums.

Fiestas also vary among the pueblos in the use of clowns. Clowns are an ancient element of Pueblo religious ceremonies, representative of discontinuity and irony in the world. In some villages they are absent at fiesta, in some they lead dances and in some they tease visitors. Often they are the most colorfully dressed and painted of the participants. At Picuris on San Lorenzo Day, August 10, for example, the clowns wear stripes of gray and black body paint, breechcloths, skull caps with corn-husk horns and necklaces made of plastic fruit or glazed doughnuts.

Special fiesta customs differ as widely as the role of clowns. Jemez features the playful Pecos Bull on August 2, when residents celebrate the patron saint of the extinct Pecos pueblo, whose survivors moved to Jemez. A man wearing a wooden frame covered with black cloth, with a roll of sheepskin for a face, charges around the village, pursued by boys whose faces are painted black. The big event at Picuris is the retrieval of a sheep carcass from the top of a 40-foot pole on August 10. Taos also has a pole climb on San Geronimo Day, September 30, along with a ritual relay race to sacred stones.

Dates for the Pueblo fiestas are:

January 23	San Ildefonso
May 1	San Felipe

June 13	Sandia
June 24	San Juan
July 14	Cochiti
July 25–26	Santa Ana
August 2	Jemez
August 4	Santo Domingo
August 9–10	Picuris
August 12	Santa Clara
August 15	Zia
August 28	Isleta ("Big Feast")
September 2	Acoma
September 4	Isleta ("Little Feast")
September 19	Laguna
September 30	Taos
October 4	Nambe
November 12	Jemez and Tesuque
December 12	Pojoaque

Other Pueblo Dances

Pueblo ceremonies are not limited to annual fiestas. Many of the pueblos have dances on Kings' Day (January 6), Easter and Christmas. Almost weekly during the rest of the year there is a ceremonial event in one or more of the pueblos, though some events are closed to visitors and some are scheduled only a short time in advance. For information on events planned for particular days, call the Santa Fe Convention and Visitor Bureau (505/984-6760), the Eight Northern Indian Pueblos Council (505/852-4265), the Six Sandoval Indian Pueblos (505/465-2255) or the governors' offices of individual pueblos. The Pueblos are not always efficient at answering phones or providing tourist information, but patience, politeness and persistence are often rewarded. Expect starting times to be approximate and be prepared to wait.

Christmas in Santa Fe

Christmas is a special time in Santa Fe because of the city's special decorations and the preservation of old Spanish folk customs. Residents outline homes and businesses with *farolitos*, traditionally made with a candle anchored in sand inside a small paper bag. Many businesses have gone to electric *farolitos*, with light bulbs and plastic bags, but few people resort to such convenience at home. The soft, warm lighting provided by the *farolitos* is often supplemented by roaring *luminarias*, bonfires made from carefully-stacked logs. The *luminarias* represent the fires of Bethlehem shepherds and are traditionally lighted on Christmas Eve, when the favorite local activity is walking or driving through the most brightly decorated neighborhoods, particularly along Canyon Road and Acequia Madre.

Luminarias also blaze on other nights preceding Christmas outside homes participating in the Las Posadas pageant. Based loosely on a sixteenth-century Spanish miracle play, Las Posadas is a reenactment of Mary and Joseph's quest for shelter. There are as many extant versions of the ritual as there are parish churches in Santa Fe, but they all start with a mass, followed by a procession to the home of a parishioner who is serving as host for the evening. There the parishioners playing Mary and Joseph entreat for shelter. The host refuses repeatedly before inviting everyone in for food and Christmas carols. Simple but powerful, the pageant is performed in Spanish by most of the local parishes for nine nights starting on December 16. One of the more elaborate versions is staged on the plaza by the Museum of New Mexico a few nights before Christmas. The museum's production includes shepherds, livestock and even Lucifer.

Occasionally a local group will also present Los Pastores, another Spanish miracle play that was very popular in Santa Fe in past centuries. Melodic folk tunes, rhyming verses and antiquated Spanish words characterize the play, which focuses on the shepherds who make the journey to Bethlehem. In New Mexican folk versions, the shepherds offer local gifts in the adoration scene—dishes of tamales, *milagros* (little charms), herbs and woolen fleeces.

PART THREE

THE
BEST
PLACES

Chapter Thirteen

♦ ♦ ♦ ♦ ♦ ♦ ♦ ♦ ♦ ♦ ♦ ♦ ♦ ♦

Hotels and Inns

FOR LODGING in Santa Fe, smaller is usually better. The large hotels and motels are more likely to provide a swimming pool and television set, and they usually offer more services for business travelers, but once you are in your room in a typical large establishment you might as well be in Omaha. With only a few important exceptions, the large hotels and motels lack local character.

For the full Santa Fe experience, visitors should reserve well in advance at one of the inns or resorts described in the first two sections below, "Top Dollar Recommendations" and "Top Value Recommendations." Though these places differ substantially in amenities, prices and styles, they all have special character. The "Top Dollar" options are good choices when cost is less important than a grand setting, but these hotels are not necessarily more polished than the "Top Value" in basics such as accommodations, food, service and ambience.

If you plan your trip too late to find room at the inn, or just prefer a "no surprises" place, the best of the standard selections are noted below by area of town. A central accommodations hotline, at 505/986-0043, operates from 8:00 to 5:00 year-round and until 10:00 P.M. summer evenings for anyone stranded.

Rates quoted are for the summer of 1993. Prices generally drop twenty to thirty percent from November through March except during holiday periods. Be sure to ask about package discounts, weekday rates, shoulder season values, or other special deals. Smoking is generally allowed only outside at the B&Bs; policies restricting it at larger establishments are mentioned in the text. The zip code for all addresses is 87501 unless otherwise noted.

Top Dollar Recommendations

THE BISHOP'S LODGE. There is a lovely passage in Willa Cather's *Death Comes for the Archbishop* when the prelate is retiring from his duties in Santa Fe. He and a long-time companion ride north from the city on horseback, up the big hill that separates Santa Fe from the Tesuque Valley. At the top of the hill they part, the companion returning to town and the archbishop continuing on to his retirement estate in the valley. This beautiful inn, about three miles from the plaza, was his destination.

At the time, Bishop Lamy had only a small adobe house and a chapel on the land. After his death Joseph Pulitzer bought the property and built two large summer homes for his daughters and their families. When the family of Jim Thorpe purchased the place in 1918, they left the chapel as it was when the archbishop died and converted the summer homes into two of the resort's luxurious lodges.

Luxury in this case has lots of casual New Mexico flavor. Many of the rooms contain viga ceilings and small corner fireplaces, used on chilly mountain nights even in the summer. The least expensive quarters tend to be a bit standard, but all rooms enjoy elements of Southwestern decor.

The Lodge has its own stables and over a thousand acres of riding trails. There are four tennis courts, with a resident professional and a pro shop, a trap and skeet shooting range with expert instruction, and a fitness center. The swimming pool, pleasantly located in the center of activity, is supplemented by a whirlpool bath and saunas.

In the summer a special children's program can be included in the rates for a family. Kids from four to twelve are picked up early in the morning for a day of supervised play, and are entertained again in the evening with puppet and magic shows.

The summer family rates also include two meals a day. The cooking is not the main reason for staying at the Lodge, but the management seems more concerned about the quality of food these days. Though there are occasional New Mexican specialties, the food is generally a combination of American and Continental. Many locals frequent the restaurant because of its superb setting and its wide buffet selection at breakfast and lunch.

Rates for a double in July and August are $170 to $375. A family of four on the plan that includes breakfast, dinner and the children's program pays from $405 to $625 per night. The rates drop other months, and the children's program is not available. The Lodge is closed from January through March. Bishop's Lodge Road, Tesuque, 505/983-6377. No credit cards.

DOS CASAS VIEJAS. Santa Fe's most delightful lodging surprise is hidden behind a gate along residential Agua Fria Street. An intimate inn with a half-dozen stunning rooms, Dos Casas Viejas is the one B&B operation competing with the city's most luxurious hotels.

A creation of Jois and Irving Belfield, it comprises two

adjacent adobe homes in a walled compound restored to 1860s character. While the architecture and antique furnishings return you to the past, the amenities are state-of-the-art. Along with a fireplace, original vigas, Mexican-tiled floors and a private walled patio, you get a phone, cable TV, gracious hospitality and an ambience of relaxed sophistication. A heated 40-foot lap pool adjoins the comfortable main parlor and dining terrace, where the hosts serve the complimentary Continental breakfast. You'll want a car for other meals and getting around town. Rates run from $125 to $185. 610 Agua Fria Street, 505/983-1636. MC, V.

INN OF THE ANASAZI. Robert Zimmer, one of the visionaries who shaped the prestigious Rosewood hotels group, opened the Inn of the Anasazi in 1991 to immense fanfare. The inn hasn't lived up to the publicity at our press deadline, well over a year later, but it's certainly matching the standards of its closest competitors and clearly has the potential to surpass them in the future.

Though only steps from the plaza, the Anasazi shutters its guests from the bustle and noise behind massive wooden doors, enveloping you in a tranquil, design-conscious Southwestern milieu. Carefully selected art graces the public areas and extends into the accommodations as well.

The 51 guest rooms and 8 suites are smaller than you expect for the price, but they come with gaslit fireplaces, four-poster beds and traditional viga-and-latilla ceilings. The least expensive quarters begin at $225 but you really need to step up to the $255 rooms for the full experience. Junior and master suites are $365 and $395 respectively. Restaurant prices keep pace with the room rates for ambitious contemporary Southwestern fare. 113 Washington Avenue, 800/688-8100, 505/988-3030. AE, MC, V.

LA POSADA. Spread out over six landscaped acres near the plaza, La Posada is closer in style and appearance to the Tesuque resorts than any of the other downtown hotels. Although each of the rooms is different, and some are fairly conventional, many of them are romantically Southwestern. The *casitas* have adobe fireplaces, exposed vigas and skylights, and they are decorated with Indian rugs and hand-painted tiles. Unfortunately, the charm in the accommodations and setting doesn't always extend to staff service, which seems to us a little lackadaisical at times.

The center of the complex is the Staab House, a Victorian mansion built in 1882, where the restaurant and lounge are located. The restaurant serves a hearty breakfast, with both New Mexican and American specialties. The elegant Victorian lounge, with overstuffed chairs, crystal chandeliers and leather barstools, is one of the most popular saloons in town. In warm weather both drinkers and diners can move outside to a lovely courtyard.

The least expensive rooms, which we don't recommend, are $130 for a single or double. *Casitas* start at $150 and go up to $330. If you can afford the high-end choices, you're likely to love La Posada. 330 E. Palace, 800/727-5276, 505/983-6351. AE, MC, V.

RANCHO ENCANTADO. The "Enchanted Ranch" is about eight miles north of Santa Fe, in the same valley that houses The Bishop's Lodge and the small village of Tesuque. The Rancho spreads out across piñon-dotted hills that afford a grand view of the Jemez Mountains and the sunset. The enchanted setting has enticed such guests as Princess Grace and Prince Rainier of Monaco, Nelson Rockefeller, Maria Callas, John Wayne and Robert Redford.

The 32 rooms of the intimate inn are among the most attractive accommodations in the Santa Fe area. All the rooms have exposed vigas and are decorated in traditional Southwestern style, with Indian rugs, hand-painted tiles and small, unobtrusive TVs. Most come with adobe fireplaces and a stacked supply of fragrant piñon pine.

The contemporary condominiums added nearby in recent years share much of the charm, and have the advantage of full kitchens and living rooms and one or two separate bedrooms. The Betty Egan House, a four-bedroom home with sweeping views, is a special spot for a larger group.

Owners John and Deborah Egan emphasize a relaxed style of gracious service at the Rancho, but they also provide all the outdoor activities anyone could desire. There are escorted trail rides into the Sangre de Cristo Mountains, hiking trails, a hilltop swimming pool and hot tub (covered in winter), tennis courts and more. The restaurant's food quality has varied over the years but the wonderful views are a constant, from either the front patio or the inside dining room.

Rates in the main lodge start at $175. A *casita* with living room or a luxury suite is $245. The condominiums range from $125 for a locked-off bedroom (without kitchen) to $300 for up to four people in a two-bedroom apartment. Route 592, Tesuque, 505/982-3537. AE, MC, V.

VISTA CLARA HEALTH RETREAT AND SPA. While spa facilities now flourish in many fashionable tourist destinations, Santa Fe has been slow to embrace the trend. The single full-service spa in the area, Vista Clara is 23 miles southeast of the city in the small village of Galisteo.

The secluded location contributes to an air of relaxed sophistication, a mood that extends to the elegant Southwestern guest quarters. The ten rooms hold a maximum of 14 people for three- or seven-day packages that cost $1,350 and $2,695 per person respectively. Both plans cover a range of daily treats, including three creative meals, fitness classes, hikes, a massage and a second body treatment such as aromatherapy or a facial. You also get shuttle service to and from the Albuquerque airport and a wardrobe of sports clothing. The longer packages also feature a hike to Pueblo ruins and a traditional sweat-lodge ceremony. Vista Clara encourages a no-alcohol policy and allows smoking only outside. Box 111, Galisteo 87540, 800/247-0301, 505/988-8865. MC, V.

Top Value Recommendations

ALEXANDER'S INN. Alexander's, a bed-and-breakfast inn, sits in a quiet residential neighborhood within walking distance of the plaza and Canyon Road. The former home, built in 1903, has been tastefully renovated to blend modern comfort with historic charm.

A detached *casita* provides the most spacious accommodation and the highest measure of Southwestern ambience. It has a kiva fireplace and, up a winding staircase, a king-size bed. Five other rooms, more country American in decor, are in the two-story main house, a brick pitched-roof bungalow brimming with sunshine. Room 5, the former master bedroom, features a four-poster bed, a fireplace, stained glass windows and a private bath. The adjacent Room 4 is a bit smaller but compensates with a private deck overlooking the shaded yard.

An ample breakfast of homemade bread or muffins, granola, fresh fruit, juice and coffee is served in the room or on a garden veranda. Owner-manager Carolyn Delecluse, who named the inn after her young son, is a gracious and helpful hostess. For the active, she makes mountain bikes available and has guest privileges at El Gancho, a racquet and health club.

Two rooms with a shared bath are $75 each, and the *casita* is $140. The other rooms range in between in price. 529 E. Palace, 505/986-1431. MC, V.

DANCING GROUND OF THE SUN B&B. Opened at Christmas in 1991, the Dancing Ground of the Sun is a B&B that specializes in space and privacy. Each suite in the renovated four-plex has its own small kitchen and a dining area for the daily complimentary breakfasts. Three of the quarters come with cozy living rooms and fireplaces, and a couple have their own washers and dryers. All feature a fine balance between old Santa Fe allure and modern comfort in the form of conveniences such as cable televisions and phones.

An easy walk to the plaza, Dancing Ground is on the outskirts of the downtown area. Rates range from $115 to $135. Each room can accommodate three adults. 711 Paseo de Peralta, 800/645-5673, 505/986-9797. MC, V.

EL PARADERO BED AND BREAKFAST INN. Though the original building was a Spanish farmhouse, constructed on the rural outskirts of the town in the early nineteenth century, this carefully remodeled 14-room inn is close to the center of the city today, about a ten-minute walk from the plaza near Guadalupe Street. A few modern touches were added during renovation—phones for example—but El Paradero has retained the simple, eccentric character of an old adobe home.

Even the small economy rooms with shared baths are colorful, cheerful and full of light. Some of the moderately priced rooms have fireplaces and private baths, and the most expensive feature fine Mexican tile and handwoven rugs. Several open onto a peaceful communal patio. The ample complimentary breakfast includes seasonal fruit, home-baked goods, homemade jams, fresh-ground coffee and special daily entrées.

Summer rates go as low as $60, for a double with a shared bath, and as high as $130 for a couple of suites with kitchenettes in an adjacent brick Victorian house. In between is a full range of nice options, including doubles with a fireplace and private bath. 220 W. Manhattan, 505/988-1177. MC, V, but personal checks preferred.

EL REY INN. El Rey is the most pleasant motel in town and one of the best in the West. Bucking the trend toward chain-inspired homogenization, El Rey exudes individual personality and offers it at bargain rates. The rooms face a large, attractive courtyard with a fountain and low adobe walls. Inside, each chamber is different but all are immaculately maintained. Many have Indian rugs, carved furniture and tile murals, and some come with adobe fireplaces and exposed vigas. The passive-solar rooms in one wing enjoy patios overlooking a garden and the heated pool, and there are also some large apartments with kitchens.

Rates vary during the year, but are always low for the atmosphere and service. In midsummer a double is $54–$125. 1862 Cerrillos, 505/982-1931. AE, MC, V.

THE GALISTEO INN. One of the nicest country hideaways near Santa Fe, the Galisteo Inn occupies a 240-year-old hacienda set on eight serene acres. In the tiny, now somewhat arty village of Galisteo, 23 miles southeast of Santa Fe, the inn provides a relaxing combination of bucolic beauty and spacious comfort.

The carefully restored adobe home features hand-hewn vigas, kiva fireplaces and old plank floors. The twelve guest rooms vary in amenities, but each is decorated in an authentic Southwestern style. The most expensive quarters contain private baths, king-size beds and sitting areas, while the least expensive have twin beds and shared baths. Some face a pasture where horses graze, and others overlook the 50-foot heated pool, which is open from

May to October. A sauna, outdoor hot tub and mountain bikes are included in the rates, along with a Continental breakfast. Massages and horseback riding are available for an extra charge. The fixed-price dinners served Wednesday through Sunday evenings are often innovative and enticing.

Rates range from $55 to $165 for the gem called Cottonwood. Box 4, Galisteo 87540, 505/982-1506. MC, V.

GRANT CORNER INN. Unusual among the distinctive places to stay in Santa Fe, the Grant Corner Inn is more European than New Mexican in flavor. Just two blocks from the plaza in a converted turn-of-the-century home, the hospitable Walter family offers 11 rooms of varying sizes and rates, each furnished with antiques. Old-fashioned quilts, armoires and brass and four-poster beds sit comfortably with such modern appliances as cable televisions, phones and ceiling fans. Five of the rooms have private baths and the other six share three baths, conveniently located.

The breakfast included with the room, which is also served to non-guests with reservations, is one of the best morning meals in Santa Fe. The selections range from banana waffles to New Mexican soufflé and always include fresh fruit, fresh-squeezed juice and homemade rolls and jellies. Guests also get complimentary wine in the evening.

Summer rates start at $65 for a small single and go up to $130 for a deluxe double. Two additional rooms are available five blocks away at the Grant Corner Inn Hacienda, a Southwestern-style condominium, for $105 and $110. 122 Grant Avenue, 505/983-6678. MC, V.

HACIENDA RANCHO DE CHIMAYÓ. About 25 miles north of Santa Fe in the mountain village of Chimayó, the Hacienda Rancho de Chimayó shares ownership and ambience with the acclaimed Restaurante Rancho de Chimayó, directly across the street. Like the restaurant, the inn was converted from a nineteenth-century rural hacienda. It lost nothing of its comfort or authenticity in the translation. Each of the seven guest rooms opens onto an enclosed courtyard, in the traditional manner. The rooms are spacious, encompassing a pleasant sitting area and a private bath, and all are furnished with regional antiques, mostly from the Victorian era. Some have a private balcony and all come with fireplaces and phones. The complimentary Continental breakfast includes fresh fruit and fresh-squeezed juice.

Rates start around $50 for the smallest single and go up to $85 for the largest double. The Hacienda is closed in early January. P.O. Box 11, Chimayó 87522, 505/351-2222. AE, MC, V.

HOTEL ST. FRANCIS. The St. Francis is the 1986 reincarnation of the old De Vargas Hotel, originally built in the 1880s. The first hotel burned in a spectacular fire, and the present structure was erected in 1924. It was a grand place for the next couple of decades, the primary gathering spot for state politicians, but it had faded substantially by the 1980s, when a group of investors restored its simple but romantic elegance.

Each of the 83 rooms is different, though most feature high ceilings and casement windows. They are furnished with brass and iron beds, fluffy comforters and period pieces. Bathroom fixtures include porcelain pedestal sinks and the original style of hexagonal tile. Afternoon tea is served in the spacious lobby. A good choice for small business conferences among the recommended hotels, the St. Francis offers a variety of meeting rooms and a convenient downtown location. The light-filled restaurant is among the best hotel dining rooms in town.

Rates are $80 to $155 for a single, $95 to $170 for a

double and $200 to $300 for suites. The least expensive rooms are quite small. 210 Don Gaspar, 505/983-5700. AE, MC, V.

HOTEL SANTA FE. The newest of the city's big hotels, the Hotel Santa Fe distinguishes itself with reasonably priced junior suites, its most popular category of lodging. "Junior" in this case is an ideal arrangement for families, incorporating a sitting room with a sofa bed, a separate bedroom, a microwave oven and an honor bar. About three-quarters of the hotel's accommodations are these or larger suites. All the quarters come with the usual comforts and Santa Fe decor, and some have balconies, a feature you should request in advance if desired.

The hotel keeps costs down by dispensing with a regular restaurant and room service. A small deli provides simple but hearty breakfasts, which guests enjoy at tables in the handsome and spacious Southwestern-style lobby, where you can also sip cocktails in the evening around a majestic fireplace.

The tribal government of the Picuris Pueblo owns and manages the Hotel Santa Fe in partnership with a group of local entrepreneurs. Many of the employees are Picuris natives, and they try to treat you as they would if they were welcoming you to their home.

The hotel sits at a busy intersection on the fringes of downtown, but you seldom notice the traffic on the other side of the wall from your room or even from the pool and Jacuzzi. Junior suites run $160 in high season, with smaller and larger accommodations ranging from $125 to $205. 1501 Paseo de Peralta at Cerrillos Road, 800/ 825-9876, 505/982-1200. AE, MC, V.

INN ON THE ALAMEDA. A few blocks from the plaza, the 36-room Inn on the Alameda blends New Mexican style with modern comfort and service. Small enough to feel intimate, large enough to have a 24-hour switchboard and new enough to have a Jacuzzi, the hotel is a good choice for anyone from a harried executive to a romantic couple. Owners Joe and Kathy Schepps see that the staff is among Santa Fe's most attentive.

The rooms combine Southwestern accents with standard hotel design, including all of the usual conveniences. The most attractive space is a large sitting room–library, just off the main entrance, where guests can enjoy a bountiful complimentary Continental breakfast in the morning and a private bar in the evening. The Executive Conference Room holds up to thirty people boardroom-style or up to one hundred theatre-style.

Rates in season range from $145 for a single to $330 for the top suite. Regular doubles are $155. 303 E. Alameda, 505/984-2121. AE, MC, V.

LA FONDA HOTEL. An inn called La Fonda was well-established on this site, adjacent to the plaza, before the opening of the Santa Fe Trail. At the time of the American occupation in 1846, the inn became the U.S. Hotel, where guests paid one dollar a day for room and board but sometimes had to sleep on and under the billiard tables in the lobby when the town was crowded.

The present building dates from 1920, though it has been enlarged several times since then. It was planned and designed by a group of local investors to reflect the historical traditions of the city in architecture and furnishings. The investors fell short of money, however, and sold the property to the Fred Harvey Company, one of the earliest large-scale promoters of Western tourism. For several decades, until the area was readily accessible to individual motorists, La Fonda was the grand station for tours of the Pueblo country. Elegant dinners were served in the evening to affluent guests, while Indians danced in the lobby. Locally owned again, the atmosphere is now more reflective of local informality than of grand touring.

Many of the rooms are thoroughly Santa Fe in decor, with Spanish colonial furniture, beamed ceilings and, in some cases, adobe fireplaces. The lobby, virtually a local monument, is a popular gathering spot. The rooftop lounge and restaurant have grand views and the swimming pool is heated.

The summer rates start at $135 for a single and $145 for a double. Several expensive suites are also available. 100 E. San Francisco, 505/982-5511. AE, MC, V.

PLAZA REAL. The same hotelier who originally made La Posada and the St. Francis such special places, Mike Cerletti, opened the Plaza Real in the summer of 1990. It's another success, this time in a territorial style at a great location just off the plaza.

All the rooms overlook a narrow courtyard, some from small balconies, and they blend local flavor smartly with contemporary comfort. The junior and master suites, which enjoy fireplaces, are especially delightful. The staff is well-trained, maintaining the service standards and the mood on a felicitous level.

Cerletti and his partners keep the prices in the 56-room establishment commendably moderate, ranging from $115 to $165. There's no restaurant on the premises, but you get a Continental breakfast in the morning and light snacks later in the day. Numerous restaurants are a quick walk. 125 Washington at Nusbaum, 800/279-7325, 505/ 988-4900. AE, MC, V.

PRESTON HOUSE. George Preston, the law partner of a notorious land speculator, built this house in 1886. The only surviving example of Queen Anne architecture in the city, the house reflects popular Anglo tastes of the late nineteenth century, when adobe was considered dirty. Several decades later, when adobe was back in fashion, the brick facade was covered with stucco to blend with the rest of the local environment.

Now an artfully converted bed-and-breakfast inn just a few blocks from the plaza, the Preston House offers a range of accommodations. Eight rooms in the original home are tastefully furnished in period style. Seven additional quarters, more Southwestern in character, occupy an adobe compound directly across diminutive Faithway Street. A pair of rooms in the main house share a bath, but the others have private facilities. Five chambers come with fireplaces and all have phones.

The least expensive room, with a shared bath, is $55. At the top end of the rates, large rooms and suites with a fireplace run from $105 to $128. Two of the suites can sleep up to four people. All guests get an elaborate Continental breakfast and full afternoon tea. Smoking is not permitted, and there is a resident cat. 106 Faithway Street, 505/982-3465. AE, MC, V.

PUEBLO BONITO. A little farther from the center of town, Pueblo Bonito Bed and Breakfast Inn is a ten-minute walk from the plaza, serenely secluded from the nearby bustle behind massive adobe walls. Converted from a small apartment complex that was originally a turn-of-the-century estate, the inn offers 15 cozy Southwestern *casitas* with kiva-style corner fireplaces, private baths, small kitchens and handmade regional furnishings. Some have hand-hewn vigas, and a few second-floor quarters enjoy views of the mountains. A handful contain sofa beds and can accommodate up to four people.

Herb and Amy Behm serve a Continental-breakfast buffet with fresh fruit, fresh-squeezed juice, cereal and homemade breads in the sunny dining room or on a pleasant central terrace, where guests also sip afternoon tea later in the day. The cost is $95 to $130. 138 W. Manhattan at Galisteo, 505/984-8001. MC, V.

TERRITORIAL INN. Tree-lined Washington Avenue, which runs a few short blocks from the plaza to the edge of the downtown district, was once a street of grand homes. The only residence left today among the restaurants and shops is occupied by the Territorial Inn, the attractive creation of owner-manager Lela McFerrin.

Most of the ten guest rooms in the 100-year-old house are up a quaint winding stairway. Two have fireplaces, as does the living room, and eight have private baths. All are tastefully furnished and come with phones and cable television. The complimentary Continental breakfast is delivered to your door, if you wish, or enjoyed in a tranquil garden with a gazebo-enclosed hot tub.

A cozy room with a queen-size bed and shared bath costs $80 year-round. You can spend up to $140, which gets you a king-size bed, fireplace and private bath. The rates are slightly higher at Indian Market and Christmas, when the location makes this a particularly good choice. 215 Washington Avenue, 505/989-7737. MC, V.

Other Downtown Hotels and B&Bs

Eldorado Hotel (309 W. San Francisco, 800/955-4455, 505/988-4455), is among the most luxurious lodging options in town. A member of the Clarion chain, and eminently comfortable and commodious, the hotel is, unfortunately, a bit out of scale for Santa Fe. An effort was made to harmonize with local styles, but Eldorado's bulk and boxiness undermine the intent. The management makes its amends with good service, fine food at The Old House, and a commendable level of community involvement. A regular double in the summer costs $225, and suites start at $285. AE, MC, V.

The Inn at Loretto (211 Old Santa Fe Trail, 800/727-5531, 505/988-5531), a Best Western hotel, was more successful in blending with the local environment. Built on the site of the old Loretto Academy, which was established by Bishop Lamy in the 1850s, the hotel still maintains the lovely Loretto Chapel that served the former school. When the inn was completed in 1975 it became an instant city landmark, the only large building constructed in recent years that effectively conceals its size through Spanish Pueblo recesses and terraces. Rooms have the expected Best Western amenities and some contemporary Southwestern design touches. The covered terrace adjacent to the swimming pool is popular with locals for lunch or late afternoon margaritas. Rates for a double are $150 to $165. The least expensive suites are $300. AE, MC, V.

The Inn of the Governors (234 Don Gaspar, 505/982-4333), also combines Southwestern decor with modern functionalism. Many of the rooms are handsome, but the ones facing Alameda can be noisy on weekend nights. The Mañana Bar is a popular watering hole. Prices run from $135 for a double to $225 for a mini-suite. AE, MC, V.

The Santa Fe Hilton Inn (100 Sandoval, 800/336-3676, 505/988-2811), is much like Hiltons elsewhere, including its rates ($130 to $245 for a double). In recent years the hotel has successfully incorporated many elements of local flavor. AE, MC, V.

A more intimate choice nearby is the Water Street Inn (427 W. Water, 505/984-1193), a B&B. Surrounded by commercial businesses, including Vanessie's restaurant just next door, the inn is a quick four blocks from the plaza. The architectural style is more contemporary than at most B&Bs in town, though the sophisticated interior decor takes you back to a more romantic era. Several of the seven rooms have private balconies or decks, most come with a four-poster bed and a fireplace or antique wood stove, and all offer private baths, air conditioning, cable TVs and phones. Rates range from $105 to $130. MC, V.

Across downtown, a similar distance from the plaza, the Inn on the Paseo (639 Paseo de Peralta, 505/984-8200) is a B&B built out of two former homes. From the street the property looks small, but it includes 19 rooms on several levels terraced down a hillside. Although the quarters contain elements of Southwestern character, as well as four-poster beds with the owner's handmade quilts, the overall feeling is one of simple, clean lines and contemporary comfort. All the rooms come with private baths, TVs and phones, and most have private entrances. Expect to pay between $90 and $140, depending on the features you get. MC, V.

Slightly closer to the plaza, the Inn of the Animal Tracks (707 Paseo de Peralta, 505/988-1546) is a homier, more traditional B&B, where you'll find comfortable clutter, a dog, two cats and five cozy rooms priced from $85 to $110.

Other downtown B&Bs include the Adobe Abode (202 Chapelle, 505/983-3133) and El Farolito (514 Galisteo, 505/988-1631), both in converted homes with a handful of rooms each. Some of El Farolito's quarters contain kitchenettes. Rates at both hover around $100, although the Abode's least expensive room is $10 cheaper and the largest of El Farolito's costs $125. MC, V for both.

The Picacho Plaza Hotel (750 N. St. Francis Drive, 505/982-5591), situated on a hill overlooking the city, about two miles from the plaza, offers amenities similar to the other large hotels. The Picacho rents out the adjacent Cielo Grande condominiums as well. The hotel rates range from $113 for a room to $178 for a parlor suite. A one-bedroom condo goes for $145 and a two-bedroom, for up to four people, for $195. AE, MC, V.

Condominiums

Condominium rentals are available in many areas of Santa Fe, but the best for most visitors are convenient to downtown. The following offer conventional condo luxury and spaciousness with a good measure of Santa Fe style.

Otra Vez en Santa Fe (Galisteo and Water, 505/988-2244), is just a couple of blocks off the plaza. One-bedroom units go for $135 in the summer and two-bedroom apartments are $25 higher. Fort Marcy Compound (320 Artist Road, 505/982-9480), is a larger, older complex. It's a little farther from the center, but still within walking distance. Rates for one and two bedrooms range from $125 to $163 for a couple, and reach $220 for four people in a three-bedroom unit.

Pueblo Hermosa (501 Rio Grande, 800/274-7990, 505/984-2590) is a similar distance from the plaza, but a step up in contemporary elegance. Views from the balconies of the more expensive units are terrific. A two-bedroom condo costs $195–$235, while the three-bedroom units run $235–$285.

Zona Rosa (429 W. San Francisco, 800/955-4455, 505/988-4455) is close to its management company, the Eldorado Hotel, in location, looks and luxury. It offers one- to three-bedroom condos from $250 to $400 and access to the Eldorado's pool and other facilities.

The Arius Compound (1018½ Canyon Road, 505/982-2621), nestles cozily into its setting, in the midst of historic Canyon Road. The three one- and two-bedroom apartments rent for $115 to $165.

Other condominium possibilities, and private homes as well, are offered by The Management Group (320 Paseo de Peralta, 800/283-2211, 505/982-2823). Experienced and professional, the company knows its business and the city. If you would like to stay in a historic home, enjoy the finest vistas, or do something else special, give them a try.

Cerrillos Road Motels

Cerrillos Road is Santa Fe's motel row, a commercial strip that leads from Interstate 25 to the city's center. The most distinctive of the motels, El Rey, is described in the "Top Value Recommendations." The Alamo Lodge (1842 Cerrillos, 505/982-1841), next door to El Rey, and the Stage Coach Motor Inn (3360 Cerrillos, 505/471-0707), farther toward the south edge of the city, have friendly managements and offer a dose of charm from the era before chains dominated the motel industry. Plan to pay $55–$60 at the Alamo and $10–$15 less at the Stage Coach, where smoking is not permitted in the rooms.

Other relatively inexpensive, reasonably attractive independents are the Thunderbird Inn (1821 Cerrillos, 505/983-4397), the Western Scene (1608 Cerrillos, 505/983-7484), and the Desert Chateau (1622 Cerrillos, 505/983-7976). Like the motels described above, the three date to a generation ago. The Thunderbird offers a courtyard swimming pool next to its $40 rooms. The other two places are jointly-owned and a touch spiffier, with rates of $55. Some of the rooms have kitchens.

More modern motel style can be found at a couple of independents as well. The Santa Fe Budget Inn (725 Cerrillos, 505/982-5952), isn't as cheap as it sounds, but it's close to downtown and has a diminutive swimming pool and satellite TV. Doubles are $75 to $85. Even closer to downtown, but without a pool, the smaller Santa Fe Motel (510 Cerrillos, 505/982-1039) charges $70 to $80 for regular rooms, an extra $5 for one with a kitchenette and $10 more for pleasant *casitas*.

The rest of the good options along Cerrillos are members of chains or associations. Two are a part of the Best Western group: the High Mesa Inn (3347 Cerrillos, 505/473-2800), which charges $95 for a double, and the smaller Lamplighter (2405 Cerrillos, 800/767-5267, 505/471-8000), where a similar but older room goes for $65 to $70. Both have indoor pools and Jacuzzis.

The least expensive chain properties are two Motel 6 operations (3007 Cerrillos, 505/473-1380, and 3695 Cerrillos, 505/471-4140), each $38. Other chains represented in town include Ramada Inn, Travelodge, Luxury Inns, Holiday Inn, Quinta Real, and Quality Inn. All keep their high-season rates under $100 and may offer substantial discounts in slower periods. Call 800/555-1212 for a toll-free telephone number for the chain's reservation office.

Other Motels

If you want condominium-like accommodations but don't want to sacrifice hotel services, consider The Residence Inn by Marriott (1698 Galisteo, 800/331-3131, 505/988-7300). The all-suites operation is a short drive from downtown near St. Vincent Hospital, off St. Michael's Drive. The attractively landscaped grounds and swimming pool provide diversions for both kids and adults. Rates are $155–$195.

The only motel on Old Pecos Trail, the most scenic entrance to the city, is the Pecos Trail Inn (2239 Old Pecos Trail, 505/982-1943). Situated along the road but on five piñon-dotted acres, the 1950s structure has been spruced up by the latest owners. Be sure to ask for a renovated room, full of handcrafted Southwestern furnishings, at $69-$76. Some of the quarters contain kitchenettes. Peppers Restaurant, adjacent and jointly-owned, provides hearty New Mexican meals popular with locals.

Chapter Fourteen
◆◆◆◆◆◆◆◆◆◆◆◆◆

Restaurants

THE NATIVE New Mexican food of Santa Fe, served in half of the local restaurants, is a piquant expression of the city's living heritage. Santa Fe's long isolation from the rest of Hispanic America produced a distinctive style of local cooking, simple in ingredients but wonderfully spicy. The native food differs notably from any of the regional cuisines of Mexico, from Tex-Mex cooking and, most especially, from the elegant fare that is currently trendy as Southwestern cuisine.

The dominant ingredient of New Mexican food is the *chile* pepper, which is much more closely related to the tomato plant than to the shrub that produces black pepper. Native to tropical America, chile has been grown under irrigation in New Mexico for at least four hundred years. When harvested the chile pods are generally green and are used in that form, chopped in small pieces, in some dishes. Or the pods can be dried, after they are a mature red, and then ground to make another kind of sauce. Many dishes served in Santa Fe restaurants can be made with either green or red chile, depending on the preference of the customer. Both versions can be hot or mild, varying with the particular chiles used, but neither will be bland.

The other basic ingredients of New Mexican meals are tortillas, pinto beans, *posole* and *sopaipillas*. Tortillas and beans are common in all forms of Mexican cooking, but they are prepared somewhat differently in New Mexico. The beans are seldom refried, which is the most typical treatment elsewhere, and the tortillas are frequently made from a special blue cornmeal that was rarely found outside the area until recently. *Posole*, a type of hominy cooked with chile and pork, is usually served instead of Spanish rice. *Sopaipillas* are a form of fried bread, often eaten with the entrée, covered with honey. Cheese, chicken, pork or beef are included in most meals in some fashion, but normally are a secondary flavor.

If you want to learn how to prepare the local dishes at home, try the Santa Fe School of Cooking (116 W. San Francisco in the Plaza Mercado, 505/983-4511). The school also has a shop for regional food products, which can be found as well at the Chile Shop (109 E. Water, 505/983-6080), and the Coyote Cafe General Store, (132 W. Water, 505/982-2454). The most useful cookbooks are Huntley Dent's *The Feast of Santa Fe* (Simon & Schuster, 1985) and our own *Rancho de Chimayó Cookbook: The Traditional Cooking of New Mexico* (Harvard Common Press, 1991).

Even the best New Mexican cooking in Santa Fe is fairly inexpensive. It's difficult to spend more than $10 a person on a meal, including drinks and dessert, and it's easy to be satisfied for $6 or less. Long waiting lines, frequently encountered in the summer, are the only reasonable excuse for not having the native food at least once a day.

There are alternatives, however, and some that are very special. The most impressive of these in food quality, along with the leading New Mexican restaurants, are described below in the sections on "Top Dollar Recommendations" and "Top Value Recommendations." These places vary considerably in atmosphere, service and price, from a super hamburger joint to a nationally chic Southwestern cafe. The "Top Dollar" options are good choices when cost is less important than a sophisticated menu and a cosmopolitan air, but these restaurants are not necessarily better than the "Top Value" recommendations in basics such as food flavor, kitchen consistency and service.

The other suggested restaurants, grouped by their general location, seem a little less dependable to us in one way or another, but they are solid enough to stand out among the hundreds of possibilities in the city. They are included in the recommendations over a number of popular restaurants that put their creative energies into Santa Fe charm instead of the cooking. If ambience is an important criterion to you, enjoy it with good food in one of the numerous places that offer both.

The price categories used in the restaurant descriptions are based on the cost of an entrée alone and are relative only to Santa Fe. The most expensive meal in town would be moderately priced by New York or international standards. "Expensive" in Santa Fe means entrées cost over $12. Under $6 is "Inexpensive," and in between is "Moderate." In the listings, standard abbreviations are used for credit cards.

Dress, along with service, tends to be casual almost everywhere. This helps to make most of the restaurants fine for families, though caution should be exercised in ordering New Mexican food for children.

Top Dollar Recommendations

CAFE ESCALERA. Opened in the summer of 1991, Cafe Escalera quickly jumped to the forefront of Santa Fe restaurants attempting creative contemporary cooking. One of the founding chefs, the talented Deborah Madison, left just before our press deadline, but her colleague David Tanis should be capable of sustaining the excellence. Though the kitchen gets its inspiration from around the world, Mediterranean influences often dominate the changing menu, which might offer options such as chicken saltimbocca, fresh tuna scented with Moroccan spices, seafood stew with Romescu sauce, or French lentil salad and new fingerling potatoes bathed in olive oil. The ingredients are always impeccable and the preparations are usually refined in an elemental, subtle style. The sleek dining room and attached bar can be noisy when they are full—frequently the case.

130 Lincoln, second floor, in Lincoln Place, downtown. 505/989-8188. Open for late breakfast, lunch and dinner daily. Reservations suggested for lunch and dinner. Lunch moderate, dinner expensive. MC, V.

COYOTE CAFÉ. Famous among food followers and fashionable in all circles, the Coyote Café takes a creative approach to Southwestern dishes and decor. Chef-owner Mark Miller, who established his reputation in the San Francisco Bay area, has attracted national press for the restaurant since its 1987 opening. Also the mastermind behind Washington, D.C.'s red-hot Red Sage, Miller uses historical ingredients of the Southwest in contemporary preparations featuring seafood, meats and game. The kitchen sometimes falters, particularly if Miller is out of town, but when the cooking is on track, it excels by any standards. While you shouldn't expect the sublime, you should be ready for the possibility.

Service isn't always up to the prices, but it no longer suffers as much from the pretensions of the restaurant's early years. The lively atmosphere distracts attention from the staff in any case, drawing your focus instead to the open kitchen, colorful folk art, cowhide chairs and other insignia of Southwest chic. The adjacent rooftop cantina, open in warm weather, serves casual but tasty food, and the general store downstairs offers the café's delicious breads and salsas to go.

132 W. Water, downtown. 505/983-1615. Open daily for lunch and dinner. Reservations necessary, sometimes well in advance. Moderate for lunch, expensive for dinner. MC, V.

ENCORE PROVENCE. After years of mediocre French restaurants, Santa Fe now has a true Gallic star. Chef-owner Patrick Benrezkellah combines the flavors of his native country, sterling ingredients and skills honed with Michelin-honored chef Guy Savoy. Sample at least one of the fish preparations, the restaurant's signature dishes, where the chef's considerable talents shine best. You can eat richly here but the emphasis is on light sauces, herb flavorings, and olive oil rather than butter. The setting is intimately romantic, in a converted home near downtown. Expensive and worth it.

548 Agua Fria, just outside downtown. 505/983-7470. Open for dinner nightly except Sunday. Reservations recommended. AE, MC, V.

INN OF THE ANASAZI. Described in the previous chapter on lodging, the Inn of the Anasazi features a dining room with aspirations as lofty as the hotel's. We think the menu and service take themselves a little too seriously, but if you forgive the earnestness, you'll find at least a competent version of contemporary Southwestern fare and sometimes a magnificent rendition. Many diners consider the restaurant decor elegantly earthy while others find its Chaco Canyon simulation a little overdone. The odds are good that there will be a better balance and consistency in all matters with time.

113 Washington, downtown. 505/988-3030. Open daily. Reservations advised, especially for dinner. Moderate for lunch, expensive for dinner. AE, MC, V.

LA TRAVIATA. Italian restaurants became the rage in Santa Fe in the early 1990s. Several of the choices are quite good, but La Traviata's cooking reaches the highest notes. The dishes change with the seasons, but they always showcase topnotch ingredients in skilled preparations, perhaps a portobello mushroom salad, pasta with Italian sausage and cream or pillows of ravioli stuffed with sweet potato and sage. The dining rooms are packed and noisy for Santa Fe, but the food may have you singing.

95 W. Marcy, downtown. 505/984-1091. Open for lunch Monday through Friday and dinner nightly. Reservations advised. Moderate to expensive. MC, V.

PINK ADOBE. The Pink, as locals call it, is so well-known it's often difficult to get in. For more than forty years the restaurant has offered the most intimate, cozy atmosphere of any spot in Santa Fe and a menu that is nicely balanced between New Mexican and New Orleans cooking. At lunch try the Gypsy Stew, laced with green chile, the Creole Salad Bowl, or one of the rotating daily specials. On the evening menu, the chicken enchiladas, the chile-smothered Steak Dunigan and the apple pie with rum sauce are minor masterpieces.

406 Old Santa Fe Trail, downtown. 505/983-7712. Open daily. Reservations necessary. Moderate for lunch, expensive for dinner. AE, MC, V.

PONTCHARTRAIN. Pontchartrain advertises Creole, Yucatecan and Caribbean cooking, though the majority of the dishes hail from Louisiana. The changing menu might offer crawfish ravioli, gumbo brimming with duck and andouille, cornmeal-coated fried catfish, or soft-shell crabs fried to a delicate crunch. The preparations are skilled and sophisticated, and the service staff tries hard to please. One of the most pleasant dining environments in town, eschewing chic in favor of solid, straightforward classic form.

319 S. Guadalupe, downtown. 505/983-0626. Open Tuesday through Saturday. Reservations recommended, especially for dinner. Moderate for lunch, expensive for dinner. MC, V.

SANTACAFE. Despite its cute name and trendy posture, Santacafe takes on a challenging menu with a great deal of success. The dishes tend to mix flavors from different areas of the world in intriguing combinations. The selections change seasonally, but look for items such as smoked pheasant spring rolls with a four chile dipping sauce or pork loin with plum sauce and kim chee. Located in the 200-year-old Padre Gallegos House, the restaurant seats you in sleekly simple interior rooms or, during the summer rush, in a lovely courtyard. Service tends to suffer when the restaurant is busy, the normal situation.

231 Washington, downtown. 505/984-1788. Open nightly for dinner, Monday to Friday for lunch. Reservations necessary. Lunch moderate, dinner expensive. MC, V.

Top Value Recommendations

DAVE'S NOT HERE RESTAURANT. Dave sold this neighborhood cafe a number of years ago, but he left his designer hamburgers behind. Served with a choice of green chile, fried onions, guacamole or almost anything you could want, the mountainous burgers abound with homey savor. The ground beef, with a perfect proportion of fat, is grilled precisely to order. Not only are the french fries

home-cut, they start from tasty potatoes. The New Mexican side of the menu is also good, but not the chief reason
to search the side-streets for this unpretentious spot,
where the checks are as small and friendly as the restaurant.

1115 Hickox, a few blocks south of the intersection of
Paseo de Peralta and St. Francis. 505/983-7060. Closed
Sunday. No reservations or credit cards. Inexpensive.

INDIA PALACE. One of the most consistent restaurants in
town, the India Palace also features some of the most
attentive service. The East Indian menu offers tender tan-
doori and curry dishes of varying heat, many vegetarian.
The breads are heavenly, especially those stuffed with
spinach or onion, and so are the chutneys that accompany
every meal. The lunch buffet provides a chance to sample
a number of dishes at a bargain price. If you don't want
to come downtown to eat, the food is almost as good at
the owners' newer and slightly more casual India House
at 2501 Cerrillos (505/471-2651).

227 Don Gaspar at Water, downtown. 505/986-5859.
Open daily for lunch and dinner. Inexpensive at lunch,
moderate at dinner. AE, MC, V.

MARIA YSABEL RESTAURANT. Any group of four or more
should definitely try Maria Ysabel's family-style dinner.
The feast starts with *chile con queso* and *chicharones*,
followed by a main course of *carne adovada, frijoles,
papas con chile verde* or rice and two kinds of enchiladas.
Dessert is a delicious *capirotada*, or bread pudding. The
same items and other New Mexican specialties are also
available a la carte, but somehow they taste better when
they are brought to the table in heaping platters and
bowls.

Maria Ysabel's clientele is primarily local. More visitors

have discovered the restaurant since its move downtown near the Hilton, but the atmosphere and service are still geared to the loyal crowd from the original neighborhood location. On weekends there is often live Spanish music featuring Roberto Montragon, the chef-owner's husband and former lieutenant-governor of the state.

409 W. Water, downtown. 505/986-1662. Open daily. Reservations advised. Moderate. MC, V.

RESTAURANTE RANCHO DE CHIMAYÓ. Eating at the Rancho de Chimayó is the quintessential New Mexican dining experience. Located about twenty-five miles north of Santa Fe in the village of Chimayó, the restaurant is in an old, comfortable adobe hacienda that was the ancestral home of the proprietors' family. The drive from Santa Fe is stunning, particularly at sunset, when the color of the sky is likely to match the red chile *ristras* (strings) hanging from the restaurant's roof. In the summer you dine outside on the patio; in the winter request one of the intimate interior rooms with a cozy log fire.

The food is as traditional as you find in a New Mexico restaurant. One of the local favorites is *carne adovada*, pork cooked in hot red chile, which can be ordered as an entrée separately, on a spicy combination plate or chopped in a burrito. Milder choices are the chicken *flautas*, the best around, or the *sopaipilla relleno*, a large *sopaipilla* stuffed with meat, beans and chile and topped with more chile and cheese. The *flan*, a custard caramel, may be the best version of this dish in the world. The bar serves good margaritas and a specialty called the Chimayó Cocktail, a combination of tequila and apple juice that is much better than it sounds.

Route 4, Chimayó. 984-2100 from Santa Fe or 505/351-4444. Closed Monday in the winter and the first half of January. Reservations necessary. Moderate. AE, MC, V.

THE SHED. The Shed is the most popular spot in town at lunch, the only meal served at this venerable establishment. The line starts forming by 11:30 on most days, but the wait is usually short and pleasant in the courtyard of the rambling adobe hacienda now occupied by the restaurant.

The enchiladas with blue corn tortillas are the finest in town, and the other New Mexican dishes are also top quality. The hamburger with green chile and cheese is less traditional, but full of local flavor. Daily soups and desserts are listed on a blackboard in each of the charming dining rooms. The green chile soup with potatoes is an excellent starter on a cold day.

113½ E. Palace Avenue, downtown. 505/982-9030. Closed Sunday. No reservations or credit cards. Inexpensive to moderate.

TECOLOTE CAFE. Despite an inauspicious appearance and location, Tecolote serves the best breakfast in town and, according to more than one national food writer, among the best breakfasts in the country. It's certainly one of the few American restaurants that have mastered the omelet. Tecolote's Santa Fe Omelet, filled with green chile and cheese, will open anyone's eyes. Other regional specialties include *huevos rancheros* (fried eggs on a corn tortilla covered with chile) and a breakfast burrito (scrambled eggs in a homemade flour tortilla topped with chile). Tecolote allows you to put together an excellent breakfast without chile, but that would be perverse behavior here. Most of the dishes come with a basket of homemade biscuits and blueberry muffins.

Lunch isn't quite up to the standards of the breakfast, but it is still an outstanding value. The selection is mainly New Mexican.

1203 Cerrillos Road. 505/988-1362. Closed Monday. No reservations. Inexpensive to moderate. MC, V.

TOMASITA'S CAFE. Tomasita's is an anomaly, a mass-production food factory that is reliable and first-rate. Many years ago, when it was a small neighborhood operation, the restaurant decided to limit its menu to a few New Mexican dishes. Specialization led to a perfection that is still maintained in much larger, more trendy surroundings. The Mexican and the combination plates, which are very similar, are prime choices. The portions are large and the service is fast and friendly, once you are seated. If you arrive in the thick of the lunch or dinner rush, have a leisurely margarita at the bar while you wait for a table.

500 S. Guadalupe, downtown in the old railroad depot. 505/983-5721. Closed Sunday. No reservations. Inexpensive. MC, V.

Recommended Downtown

There are several good options for New Mexican food downtown, in addition to Maria Ysabel, The Shed and Tomasita's. For breakfast, try Tia Sophia's (210 W. San Francisco, 505/983-9880), which features one of the best breakfast burritos in town, with hash browns and bacon wrapped in a flour tortilla and covered with chile. (Closed Sunday, no reservations, inexpensive, MC, V.)

Breakfast is also excellent at the Guadalupe Cafe (313 Guadalupe, 505/982-9762), though the restaurant is a fine choice for reasonably priced food any time of the day. Somehow the lunches, particularly the specials, seem to come out better than the dinners. (Closed Monday and Sunday dinner, reservations advised, inexpensive to moderate, MC, V.)

Josie's Casa de Comida (225 E. Marcy, 505/983-5311), has been a local favorite for lunch for many years. The regional dishes are superb, the standard American items are above par and the daily dessert specials are dynamite.

(Closed Saturday and Sunday, no reservations or credit cards, inexpensive.)

On the other side of downtown, near the state capitol, Rincon del Oso (639 Old Santa Fe Trail, 505/983-5337), also is great for lunch. The spicy green chile salsa is the only excuse you should need. (Closed Saturday and Sunday, open for dinner Friday evenings in the summer, no reservations except for dinner, inexpensive to moderate, no credit cards.)

For lunch or dinner, the Blue Corn Cafe (116 W. San Francisco in Plaza Mercado, 505/984-1800) accompanies its spicy fare with one of the largest collections of tequilas in town. The *taquitos* appetizer makes a good light midday meal. (Open daily, no reservations, inexpensive to moderate, AE, MC, V.)

For a quick, cheap lunch, grab a Frito pie at Woolworth (58 E. San Francisco) and eat it on the plaza, have the *fajitas* at Real Burger (227 Don Gaspar), or try Roque Garcia's world-class *carnitas* stand (corner of Palace and Washington). If you need to sit down, go to the Burrito Company (111 Washington Avenue).

La Tertulia (416 Aqua Fria, 505/988-2769), is the most formal New Mexican restaurant downtown. Located in a converted convent that exudes Santa Fe character, La Tertulia serves mild but flavorful local dishes, along with salads and sandwiches at lunch and steaks in the evening. (Closed Monday, reservations necessary, moderate to expensive, MC, V.)

If you burn out on local food, you can sample a variety of other cuisines downtown. Restaurant Thao (322 Garfield, off Guadalupe, 505/988-9562), serves Thai-inspired dishes. A limited number of tables and a caring kitchen ensure a tasty meal. (Open lunch and dinner daily except Sunday, reservations advised, moderate to expensive, MC, V.)

Shohko Cafe (321 Johnson, 505/983-7288), and Sakura (321 W. San Francisco, 505/983-5353), are the city's best Japanese restaurants, usually dependable for anything from *sashimi* to *tempura*. The *sushi* bar is much larger and livelier at Shohko (closed for lunch on weekends, reservations advised, moderate to expensive, AE, MC, V). Sakura has several *tatami* rooms (closed Sunday, reservations advised, moderate to expensive, MC, V).

For elegant Italian evenings, try Julian's (221 Shelby, 505/988-2355), with its classic regional dinners, or Babbo Ganzo (130 Lincoln, second floor, 505/986-3835), a Tuscan-style trattoria also open for lunch most days. (Reservations advised for both, expensive, MC, V.) Pranzo (540 Montezuma at Sanbusco Center, 505/984-2645) offers a more animated, casual atmosphere and lower prices. (Open daily for lunch and dinner, reservations advised, moderate to expensive, AE, MC, V.)

Vanessie of Santa Fe (434 W. San Francisco, 505/982-9966), features Gargantuan portions of grilled steak, chicken, lamb and fish, the only entrée choices, and pieces of cheesecake large enough to share with the entire table. The piano bar provides a pleasant interlude before or after getting stuffed. (Open daily for dinner only, no reservations, moderate to expensive, AE, MC, V.)

The Carry-Out Cafe at the Design Center Santa Fe (418 Cerrillos Road, two blocks east of Guadalupe, 505/984-3003), is a fine stop for a lunch or an early dinner to go, and seating is also available in the mall. The selections, which change weekly, range from Chinese delicacies to Moroccan *couscous*, prepared ably by Kristin Watson and Blue Yee. (Closed Sunday and Monday, no reservations, moderate, MC, V.)

Another good take-out alternative, The Pepper Grill (238 N. Guadalupe, 505/982-3658) specializes in Southwestern dishes. Try the blackened fish tacos or northern New Mexican casserole with chicken, green chile and pumpkin seed *mole*, both regularly on the varying menu.

The restaurant provides a small informal dining space and patio for eating there. (Closed Sunday, open Monday for lunch only, and other days for lunch and dinner, inexpensive to moderate, MC, V.)

Bagelmania (420 Catron, 505/982-8900), across the street, makes hefty deli sandwiches and bakes some of the best bagels and bialys west of the Hudson, to go or eat in. (Breakfast and lunch Monday through Saturday, Sunday brunch, bakery open until 3:00 P.M. on Sundays and 6:00 P.M. other days, inexpensive.)

Pasqual's (121 Don Gaspar, 983-9340), is very popular all hours of the day. The breakfast menu features *huevos rancheros*, standard egg dishes and pancakes, while the lunch menu offers soups, salads, sandwiches and stir-fry dishes. More elaborate but still earthy dinners are served six nights a week during the summer. (Open daily except Wednesday, no reservations, inexpensive for breakfast and lunch, moderate for dinner, AE, MC, V.)

Another local favorite, Carlos' Gospel Cafe (150 Washington, 505/983-1841) provides a funky atmosphere and gospel music to accompany the hangover (potato and corn) stew and various sandwiches. (Closed Sunday, lunch only, no reservations or credit cards, inexpensive.)

Zia Diner (326 S. Guadalupe, 505/988-7008) also packs in the populace with hearty portions of modern American cafe cooking, including meat loaf, burgers, and our favorite Cobb salad. (Open Monday through Saturday for lunch, Sunday for dinner, no reservations, moderate, AE, MC, V.)

The San Francisco Street Bar and Grill (114 W. San Francisco, 505/982-2044), specializes in burgers and stays open until 11:00 in the evening, late for Santa Fe. (Open daily, no reservations, inexpensive to moderate, MC, V.)

The best nonregional breakfast downtown is at the Grant Corner Inn (122 Grant Avenue, 505/983-6678). The Saturday and Sunday brunches are particularly wonderful, but everything is fresh and homemade any day of the week. (Open daily for breakfast only, reservations necessary for non-guests, inexpensive to moderate, MC, V.)

For espresso, cappuccino or latte, with a light snack and reading material, try Galisteo News (201 Galisteo, 505/984-1316), Downtown Subscription (376 Garcia, 505/983-3085), the Bookroom Coffeebar (616 Canyon, 505/988-5323) or Old Santa Fe Trail Books (613 Old Santa Fe Trail, 505/988-8878). All specialize in people-watching as much as coffee.

Recommended in Other Areas

There are several attractive restaurants on Canyon Road, but generally they are notable more for atmosphere than for food. The most successful kitchen is at Geronimo Lodge (724 Canyon, 505/982-1500), in the historic Borrego House. The ambitious, eclectic menu emphasizes contemporary Southwestern fare with Asian accents. (Open Tuesday through Sunday for lunch, daily for dinner, reservations advised, moderate to expensive, AE, MC, V.)

The best-known restaurant on the ancient street is The Compound (653 Canyon, 505/982-4353), the only place in northern New Mexico that requires men to wear a jacket and tie to dinner. The Continental cuisine is mediocre, but the setting is subtly sensuous. Famed designer Alexander Girard converted a nineteenth-century hacienda into a graceful dining space. (Closed Sunday lunch, all day Monday and the months of January and February, reservations necessary, expensive, AE.)

Celebrations (613 Canyon Road, 505/989-8904), a casual spot we enjoy best for breakfast or lunch, knows enough about good cooking to keep the dishes simple. (Open daily for breakfast and lunch, dinner served

Wednesday through Saturday, no reservations, moderate, AE, MC, V.)

The Tesuque Village Market, about six miles north of the Santa Fe plaza just off Bishop's Lodge Road (505/ 988-8848), provides hearty breakfasts, lunches and dinners. The homey, rustic market is away from the tourist attractions, but gets packed with visitors and locals alike who enjoy the setting. (Open daily, no reservations, inexpensive to moderate, MC, V.)

Maria's New Mexican Kitchen (near St. Francis Drive at 555 W. Cordova, 505/983-7929), is another popular operation. *Fajitas* have been the specialty for the last few years, but many people prefer the cheese and piñon tamales. (Open daily, reservations advised, inexpensive to moderate, AE, MC, V.)

The Old Mexico Grill (2434 Cerrillos, 505/473-0338) also serves *fajitas*, though most of the menu strives for Mexico City sophistication. The dining room is more attractive than the strip shopping center location leads you to believe. (Open daily, dinner only Sundays, no reservations, moderate, MC, V.)

Red Cloud Cafe (2400 Cerrillos, 505/438-8200), in the same center, attempts anything but an urbane posture with its casual setting and down-home country menu, complete with lumpy mashed potatoes. It's a good choice for families or anyone tired of "fine" food. (Open daily, no reservations, inexpensive to moderate, MC, V.) India House, mentioned previously with its sister India Palace, is across the road.

A few blocks farther south, Tortilla Flats (3139 Cerrillos, 505/471-8685) specializes in solid New Mexican fare from morning until night. The *New York Times* once touted it as the top native restaurant in Santa Fe and it's been full ever since. (Open daily, no reservations, inexpensive to moderate, MC, V.)

The freshest fish and seafood in town is at Rosedale

(907 W. Alameda, 505/989-7411), a combination restaurant and seafood market. The straightforward preparations allow the ingredients to shine. (Lunch only, closed Sunday, no reservations, moderate, MC, V.)

The seafood specials are also good at The Steaksmith at El Gancho (Las Vegas Highway off Old Pecos Trail, 505/988-3333). The real focus, however, is beef. The steaks are consistently the best in town. (Open daily dinner only, reservations advised, expensive, AE, MC, V.)

Fast Food

Santa Fe has most of the standard fast-food franchises, generally located on Cerrillos Road. Forget them until you return home and try instead some of the local and small-chain operations, where the food is almost always better.

The top options for fast native food are on or near Cerrillos. Baja Tacos (2621 Cerrillos, 505/471-8762) is directly on the main drag, and El Tamalero can be found just west of Cerrillos (1155 Siler, 505/471-0615). In season, also consider the outdoor café at Jackalope (2820 Cerrillos, 505/471-8539).

Chicago Dog Express (600 Cerrillos at Paseo de Peralta, 505/984-2798) makes splendid versions of the namesake hot dogs and a mean Frito pie too. For hamburgers head to Bert's Burger Bowl (235 N. Guadalupe, 505/982-0215). El Primo (234 N. Guadalupe, 505/988-2007), across the street, is a great choice for pizza, which the restaurant will deliver inside the city limits.

Chapter Fifteen
••••••••••••
Galleries and Shops

ARTISTS and artisans of the Santa Fe area are producing more fine work today than at any other time in the city's long history. Spending time with their creations in Santa Fe galleries and shops is both delightful and enlightening, as important in absorbing the city's heritage as walks along old, adobe-lined streets.

The abundance and quality of current work has stimulated a major gallery boom. In the past two decades the number of shops offering original art and handcrafted products from the area has leaped from a handful to well over a hundred. Today there are considerably more galleries per capita in Santa Fe than in New York City.

The downside to the shopping situation is the recent explosion of schlocky souvenir stores and nationally franchised boutiques, the kinds of tourist businesses that try to drown the special, distinctive character of popular destinations all across the globe. These shops have sprouted throughout downtown, intent apparently on making a theme park out of Santa Fe.

Savvy shoppers and browsers can find plenty of won-

derful Southwestern products to buy or just admire, but
you have to be choosy about where you look. The following is a selective list of places that carry high-quality handmade or artist-designed work. Most of them represent
local artists and artisans, but some, as noted, feature
work from elsewhere. Shops come and go, of course,
and also change personalities, so a diligent prober will
always discover new delights and erstwhile disappoint-
ments.

People who are unfamiliar with the unique cultural
heritage of the area should consult Chapters 1 to 3, or
other appropriate sources, before shopping. The earlier
chapters provide a basic orientation to the region's Indian,
Spanish and Anglo artistic traditions and mention some
of the prominent artists in each.

Galleries and shops are generally open from 10:00 to
5:00 or 6:00. Many close on Sunday and some also close
on Monday during the winter.

The area code for all telephone numbers is 505.

Indian Art and Crafts

◆ Joshua Baer and Company. 116½ E. Palace, downtown
(988-8944). Classic American Indian art.
◆ Case Trading Post. 704 Camino Lejo, in the Wheelwright Museum of the American Indian (982-4636).
Wide range of current work, plus some historical
pieces.
◆ Channing Gallery. 53 Old Santa Fe Trail (upstairs), on
the plaza (984-2133). Broad selection of fine art and
ethnographic material.
◆ Cristof's. 106 W. San Francisco, downtown (988-
9881). Navajo rugs, kachina dolls, sand paintings, bead
jewelry.
◆ Dewey Galleries. 74 E. San Francisco, on the plaza
(982-8632). Beautiful Navajo rugs and jewelry.

♦ Kania-Ferrin Gallery. 662 Canyon Road (982-8767). Kachina dolls, baskets, jewelry, textiles.
♦ Nedra Matteucci's Fenn Galleries. 1075 Paseo de Peralta (982-4631). Small selection for collectors.
♦ Morning Star Gallery. 513 Canyon Road (982-8187). Mainly historical Indian art, masks, pottery, hides. Plains tribes especially well-represented.
♦ Robert F. Nichols. 419 Canyon Road (982-2145). Pueblo pottery.
♦ Packard's Indian Trading Company. 61 Old Santa Fe Trail, on the plaza (983-9241). Wide range and large selection of current work. Excellent quality relative to price.
♦ Palace of the Governors Museum Shop, on the plaza (982-3016). Mainly Pueblo pottery and jewelry.
♦ James Reid. 114 E. Palace, downtown (988-1147). *Concha* belts, silver jewelry, Navajo rugs, Pueblo pottery.
♦ Santa Fe East. 200 Old Santa Fe Trail, downtown (988-3103). Fine jewelry and pottery.
♦ Textile Arts Gallery. 1571 Upper Canyon Road (983-9780). Museum-quality textiles selected by Mary Hunt Kahlenberg. Call for an appointment.
♦ Throckmorton Fine Arts. 550 Canyon Road (988-1698). Broad selection of old and new work.

Hispanic Art and Crafts

♦ Artesanos Imports. 222 Galisteo, downtown (983-5563). Mexican furnishings and crafts.
♦ Centinela Traditional Arts. Box 4, Centinela Ranch, on Highway 76, Chimayó (351-2180). Top-quality Rio Grande weavings, from Lisa and Irvin Trujillo and others.
♦ Claiborne Gallery. 558 Canyon Road (982-8019). Spanish colonial furnishings and religious art.

♦ Foreign Traders. 202 Galisteo, downtown (983-6441). Excellent selection of imported folk art and Mexican furnishings.
♦ Jackalope. 2820 Cerrillos Road (471-8539). Extensive market for Mexican imports, mainly inexpensive items.
♦ Davis Mather Folk Art Gallery. 141 Lincoln, downtown (983-1660). Mexican and New Mexican folk art.
♦ Montez Gallery. 125 E. Palace, #3, downtown (982-1828). High-quality New Mexican folk art and Spanish colonial collectibles.
♦ Ortega's Galeria (351-2288) and Weaving Shop (351-4215). Route 4, Chimayó. The largest selection of Rio Grande weavings from the area plus other local crafts and folk art.
♦ que tenga Bueno Mano. P.O. Box 762 (982-2912). Stunning collection of Latin American folk art and jewelry, assembled by Patricia LaFarge. By appointment only.
♦ The Rainbow Man. 107 E. Palace, downtown (982-8706). Local folk art and furnishings.
♦ Santa Fe Store. 211 Old Santa Fe Trail, downtown (982-2425). Mainly imported work, but also good local woodcarvings and handmade fiesta clothing.

Contemporary Fine Art

♦ Laura Carpenter Fine Art. 309 Read, off Guadalupe (986-9090). Sophisticated art in several media, much of it by nationally recognized artists.
♦ Copeland Rutherford Fine Art. 403 Canyon Road (983-1588). A variety of work by good but often under-recognized artists from the area.
♦ Linda Durham Gallery. 400 Canyon Road (988-1313). Primarily abstract painting and photography by nationally recognized New Mexican artists; an excellent track record for supporting adventuresome new work.

◆ Glenn Green Galleries. 50 E. San Francisco, downtown (988-4168). Exclusive representative for Indian sculptor Allan Houser.

◆ Elaine Horwitch Galleries. 129 W. Palace, downtown (988-8997). Represents a variety of successful, talented Southwestern artists. Lots of delightful imagery.

◆ Charlotte Jackson Fine Art. 123 E. Marcy, downtown (989-8688). Represents Fritz Scholder.

◆ Edith Lambert Gallery. 707 Canyon Road (984-2783). Solid range of work, much of it with a Southwestern flavor.

◆ Allene Lapides Gallery. 217 Johnson, downtown (984-0191). Primarily abstract painting and sculpture with some photography. Many nationally known names.

◆ Lewallen Fine Art. 225 Galisteo, downtown (988-5387). Represents a number of the Southwest's best contemporary Indian and Hispanic artists.

◆ Ernesto Mayans. 601 Canyon Road (983-8068). Painting, prints and photography by regional and national artists.

◆ The Munson Gallery. 225 Canyon Road (983-1657). Work in a variety of media by established contemporary realists.

◆ Peyton Wright. 131 Nusbaum, downtown (989-9888). Contemporary fine art and photography, mostly non-representational.

◆ Rettig y Martinez Gallery. 901 W. San Mateo, west of St. Francis Drive (983-4640). Diverse collection of impressive work by New Mexican and Mexican artists, including some large-scale sculpture.

◆ Scheinbaum and Russek Gallery of Photography. 328 Guadalupe, downtown (988-5116). Fine photography.

◆ Laurel Seth Gallery. 1121 Paseo de Peralta, downtown (988-7349). Contemporary Southwestern representational painting.

◆ Shidoni Gallery and Foundry. Bishop's Lodge Road,

Tesuque (988-8008). One of the best galleries in the country for large-scale sculpture, plus work in other media.

♦ Andrew Smith Gallery. 76 E. San Francisco (upstairs), on the plaza (984-1234). Nineteenth- and twentieth-century photography, much of it by well-known local artists.

♦ Riva Yares Gallery. 231 Washington, downtown (984-0330). Paintings and sculpture, primarily nonrepresentational.

Traditional Fine Art

♦ Cline Gallery. 526 Canyon Road (982-5328). Founders of Taos and Santa Fe art colonies, New Mexico Modernists and contemporary work.

♦ Dewey Galleries. 74 E. San Francisco, on the plaza (982-8632). Fine representational painting.

♦ Nedra Matteucci's Fenn Galleries. 1075 Paseo de Peralta (982-4631). Paintings by the Founders of the Taos and Santa Fe art colonies and other artists working in similar styles.

♦ Nedra Matteucci Fine Art. 555 Canyon Road (983-2731). Representational work by regional artists, living and deceased.

♦ Linda McAdoo Galleries. 503 Canyon Road (983-7182). Paintings by the Founders and their heirs.

♦ Owings-Dewey Fine Art. 74 E. San Francisco (upstairs), on the plaza (982-6244). Mainly paintings by nationally known nineteenth- and twentieth-century American artists.

♦ Gerald Peters. 439 Camino del Monte Sol, between Canyon Road and Old Santa Fe Trail (988-8961). Paintings by the Founders and contemporary representational work.

♦ Wadle Galleries. 128 W. Palace, downtown (983-

9219). Diverse collection of work by Indian and Anglo artists, primarily with Western themes.

♦ **Woodrow Wilson Fine Art.** 319 Read, off Guadalupe (983-2444). Early Taos and Santa Fe schools plus contemporary representational paintings.

♦ **Zaplin-Lambert Gallery.** 651 Canyon Road (982-6100). Paintings and prints from the nineteenth and twentieth centuries.

Contemporary Fine Crafts

♦ **Bellas Artes.** 653 Canyon Road (983-2745). Unusual ethnic styles in contemporary work.

♦ **De Bella.** 100 E. Palace, downtown (984-0692). Well-designed jewelry, primarily gold and gemstones.

♦ **Garland Gallery.** 66 W. Marcy, downtown (984-1555). Imaginative glasswork, much of it sculptural.

♦ **Gusterman Silversmiths.** 126 E. Palace, downtown (982-8972). Well-designed silver jewelry.

♦ **Jett.** 110 Old Santa Fe Trail, downtown (988-1414). Creative designs in jewelry.

♦ **Kent Galleries.** The Contemporary Craftsman. 130 Lincoln, downtown (988-1001). Wide range and large selection of fine regional crafts.

♦ **Ross Lewallen Jewelry.** 105 E. Palace, downtown (983-2657). A leading jeweler in the city for many years.

♦ **Lightside Gallery.** 225 Canyon Road (982-5501). Broad selection of crafts with some contemporary paintings.

♦ **Mariposa Santa Fe.** 225 Canyon Road (982-3032). Local branch of Albuquerque's most impressive crafts gallery.

♦ **La Mesa of Santa Fe.** 225 Canyon Road (984-1688). Handcrafted items for the table and home with Southwestern flair.

◆ Leslie Muth Gallery. 225 E. De Vargas, downtown (989-4620). Contemporary American folk art.
◆ Nambe Mills. 112 W. San Francisco, downtown (988-3574), and 924 Paseo de Peralta (988-5528). Distinctive metal cooking and serving ware made from original designs in Santa Fe.
◆ Okun Gallery. 301 N. Guadalupe, downtown (989-4300). High-quality crafts from recognized artists.
◆ Ornament. 209 W. San Francisco, downtown (983-9399). Traditional and contemporary jewelry designs.
◆ Quilts Ltd. 652 Canyon Road (988-5888). Collection-quality quilts in traditional and Southwestern styles.
◆ Running Ridge Gallery. 640 Canyon Road (988-2515). Delightful array of fine crafts, many of them sculptural, plus prints.
◆ Tesuque Glassworks. Bishop's Lodge Road, next to Shidoni, Tesuque (988-2165). Beautiful glassware direct from the studio of Charlie Miner and associates.
◆ Antony Williams Designers. 211 Old Santa Fe Trail in the Inn at Loretto, downtown (982-3443). Distinctive jewelry, many pieces with gemstones.

Home Furnishings and Architectural Crafts

◆ Acequia Gallery. 821 Canyon Road (988-1531). Rustic Southwestern handcrafted furnishings.
◆ American Country Collection. 620 Cerrillos Road (984-0955). Country furniture of various styles, some affordable reproductions.
◆ Architectural Antiques. 1125 Canyon Road (982-0042). Spanish colonial doors, fixtures and other architectural detail.
◆ Arius Tile Company. 114 Don Gaspar, downtown (988-1196). Locally made designer tiles.

- Artesanos Imports. 222 Galisteo, downtown (983-5563). Mexican ceramic tiles and sinks plus other traditional items for the home.
- Collaboration. 544 S. Guadalupe (984-3045). Southwestern furnishings by Ernest Thompson and Peter Gould and window treatments from the Sombraje Collection.
- Dell Woodworks. 1326 Rufina Circle, off Cerrillos Road (988-9612). Refined custom work in a regional style.
- Dewey Galleries. 74 E. San Francisco, on the plaza (982-8632). Mexican and New Mexican Spanish colonial furnishings.
- Foreign Traders. 202 Galisteo, downtown (983-6441). Excellent selection of Mexican furnishings.
- Volker de la Harpe Carved Doors and Furniture. 707 Canyon Road (983-4074). Contemporary and traditional designs made on site.
- Jackalope Furniture. 2810 Cerrillos Road (471-5390). Inexpensive Mexican furniture.
- Lost City Gallery. 702½ Canyon Road (986-9892). High-quality furniture, contemporary in style.
- La Mesa of Santa Fe. 225 Canyon Road (984-1688). Handcrafted items for the table and home with Southwestern flair.
- Rancho. 322 McKenzie (986-1688). Western ranch–style furnishings and collectibles.
- Southwest Spanish Craftsmen. 328 S. Guadalupe, downtown (982-1767). Carefully executed reproductions of Spanish colonial and provincial furniture, including museum pieces.
- Taos Furniture. 232 Galisteo, downtown (988-1229). "Taos-style" home furnishings.
- Umbrello. 701 Canyon Road (984-8566). Choice Southwestern furniture and tableware.

Distinctive Clothes and Accessories

◆ Char. 104 Old Santa Fe Trail, downtown (988-5969). Flashy suede and leather fashions.

◆ Little Bits. 318 Aztec, off Guadalupe (983-4149). Children's wear.

◆ Montecristi Custom Hat Works. 118 Galisteo, downtown (983-9598). Authentic Panama hats.

◆ Origins. 135 W. San Francisco, downtown (988-2323). Delightful collection of unusual women's clothes and accessories.

◆ Overland Sheepskin Company. 217 Galisteo, downtown (983-4727). Great coats and slippers made in Taos.

◆ Salamander Leathers. 78 E. San Francisco, on the plaza (982-9782). Contemporary and Western designs for men and women.

◆ Santa Fe Weaving Gallery. 124½ Galisteo, downtown (982-1737). Locally made women's clothing.

◆ Simply Santa Fe. 72 E. San Francisco, on the plaza (988-3100). Eclectic selection of clothing for women, much of it Southwestern or Native American in inspiration.

◆ Jane Smith. 122 W. San Francisco, downtown (988-4775). Custom-knit sweaters and chic Southwestern wear for men and women.

◆ Spider Woman Designs. 225 Canyon Road (984-0136). Women's clothes and decorative textiles.

◆ Ann Sterling. 125 E. Palace in Seña Plaza, downtown (984-9864). Imported handknits for men and women.

◆ Susan K's Artwear. 229 Johnson, downtown (989-8226). Women's clothing and jewelry with flair.

◆ Tom Taylor. 100 E. San Francisco, downtown (984-2231). Custom boots, belts and buckles.

◆ Yarrow Collection. 223 W. San Francisco, downtown (982-2030). Fine leather and suede clothing.

For Any of the Above and Who Knows What Else

Trader Jack's Flea Market. Highway 284/85 just beyond the Santa Fe Opera. One of the great bazaars in the Southwest, Trader Jack's attracts savvy locals and visitors alike for its value-priced, often unusual merchandise. Even if you're not searching for used cowboy boots, Guatemalan fabrics, buckles, bangles or beads, the market makes for fine people-watching, especially on weekend mornings.

Chapter Sixteen
♦♦♦♦♦♦♦♦♦♦♦♦♦
Nightlife

N O ONE lives in or visits Santa Fe because of its nightlife. When the gambling halls closed early this century and the fandango went out of fashion, a big gap was left in local entertainment. Performing arts events fill the void in the summer, but the rest of the year is lean. Anyone with determination, however, can find some form of amusement in any season. Santa Fe is not as slow or strait-laced as most American cities of its size.

Dancing

As in any city, clubs come and go. The "Pasatiempo" section of the Friday *New Mexican* is the best source of current information, though no one would call the newspaper painstakingly thorough.

Recent years have seen more shake-out than usual. The steadiest spots for live contemporary music at press time are Chez What (213 W. Alameda, downtown, 505/982-0099) and Luna (519 Cerrillos Road, near downtown, 505/989-4888). Both attract young crowds. The cover charge at either can be a little steep compared with other local clubs, but it varies with the night of the week and the prominence of the musicians.

Other downtown possibilities, particularly on weekends, include the high-tech Edge (135 W. Palace, 3rd floor, 505/986-1700), The Bull Ring, a hangout for state politicos (414 Old Santa Fe Trail, 505/983-3328), Inn at Loretto (211 Old Santa Fe Trail, 505/988-5531), Hilton Inn (100 Sandoval, 505/988-2811) and Ogelvies Bar and Grille (150 Washington at Marcy, 505/988-3855). If you want to get away from downtown in search of local haunts, try a dose of country at Rodeo Nights (2907 Cerrillos Road, 505/471-3000).

Listening Music

A variety of local musicians perform around the city on a regular or irregular basis. Again, check "Pasatiempo" for dates and places. Ruben Romero and Antonio Mendoza are fabulous classical guitarists. Pianist John Gooch is always fun, lively and very talented, too. South by Southwest plays country rock. Another group, Distilled Spirits, does Irish folk music, as does solo performer Gerry Carthy. Johnny Gilbert's a good bet for hot jazz. The most popular vocalists are Father Frank Pretto and David Salazar, both of whom feature Spanish songs, and Bill and Bonnie Hearne for country folk.

A fluctuating number of promoters bring in musicians from other parts of the country for concerts, most often in the summer. Check the paper for possibilities. If *conjunto* dynamo Flaco Jimenez is in town, as he is several times a year, don't miss him.

Bars

For a quieter evening in a pleasant setting, Santa Fe offers lots of good options. Several of the restaurants recommended in Chapter 14 have cheerful, comfortable bars, including Coyote Café, Rancho de Chimayó, and Vanessie, where the popular Doug Montgomery presides over the piano. The Pink Adobe's Dragon Room was once rated as one of the world's best bars by an international edition of *Newsweek*, joining New York's 21 Club as the only U.S. establishments on the list.

Other inviting bars, also attached to restaurants, are El Farol, (808 Canyon Road, 505/983-9912), which has *tapas* and nightly live music, El Nido (Bishop's Lodge Road in Tesuque, 505/988-4340), Palace Restaurant and Bar (142 W. Palace, 505/982-9891), Garduño's (130 Lincoln, 505/983-9797) and La Casa Seña Cantina (125 E. Palace in Seña Plaza, 505/988-9232), where young singers perform Broadway show tunes.

The most attractive hotel bars are in La Posada Inn, Inn of the Anasazi, Inn of the Governors and on top of La Fonda Hotel (see Chapter 13). For local funk and flavor, try Evangelo's (200 W. San Francisco, 505/982-9014) or the Green Onion (1851 St. Michael's Drive, 505/983-5198).

Hot Tubs

Even quieter and more relaxing is a soak under the stars. Ten Thousand Waves (505/988-1047 or 982-9304) is a Japanese bathhouse in the mountains, about three and a half miles from the plaza up the road to the Santa Fe Ski Area. Patrons don kimonos and sandals in sexually-segregated dressing areas before going to their assigned tubs, all outside. There are nine private tubs, with different views of the sunset and sky, and one communal tub for as many as two dozen people. Book on a night with a full moon for the ultimate experience.

An entirely different soaking adventure is available in Ojo Caliente, a small town about an hour north of Santa

Fe on U.S. 285. The main business in the town is an old, slightly rundown spa (505/583-2233) built around natural hot springs. The separate facilities for men and women both feature mineral water pools, arsenic baths and sweat tables. It's a different era of soaking, an interesting return to Victorian styles of health care. The spa is not open at night, but it can help wash away painful memories of the night before.

Films

Santa Fe has some two dozen movie theaters. While all the expected first-run hits play in town, what's notable is the number of artistic, experimental and foreign films. Count on the Center for Contemporary Arts (505/982-1338), described in Chapter 7, to host the most powerful and intriguing series each season. St. John's College (Camino de Cruz Blanca, 505/982-3691) offers quality cinema too, during the school year, always open to the general public.

Commercial theaters with an eye toward excellence include the Jean Cocteau (418 Montezuma near Guadalupe, downtown, 505/988-2711) and Grand Illusion (St. Michael's Village on St. Michael's Drive, 505/471-8935). Go see anything at the Lensic (211 W. San Francisco, downtown, 505/982-0301), if only to enjoy the grand old theater itself.

Santa Fe Downs

The thoroughbreds and quarter horses at the Santa Fe Downs race into the early evening from June until Labor Day. Post time is 4:00 P.M. on Wednesday and Friday and 1:30 P.M. on Saturday and Sunday. The Downs (505/471-3311) is just south of the city limits, off Interstate 25.

Chapter Seventeen

Transportation and Services

Getting to Santa Fe

ALTHOUGH there is a small airport in Santa Fe with a limited amount of commercial service, most residents and visitors use the far larger and busier airport in Albuquerque, 63 miles south. Shuttlejack (505/982-4311) operates frequent bus service from the Albuquerque airport to Santa Fe. It costs $20 one way and drops you downtown at either the Eldorado Hotel or the Inn at Loretto, or, upon advance request, at other downtown area hotels.

The best plan, however, is to rent a car. All of the major national rental agencies have offices at the airport and toll-free 800 numbers for reservations. Though most of Santa Fe can be enjoyed on foot, a car is handy for some city sights and for trips to Taos and the pueblos.

A car will also allow you to make the most of the trip from Albuquerque to Santa Fe by taking the Turquoise Trail instead of the Interstate. This backroads highway, described in Chapter 9, is the scenic route between the cities. From the airport take Interstate 25 toward Santa Fe and then go east on Interstate 40 until exit 175. Follow the signs from there to Highway 14, which you take to Santa Fe.

Santa Fe Transportation

At press time, the City of Santa Fe was starting a new bus system, Santa Fe Trails. Most routes are geared toward residents, but it can get visitors around to some sights as well. Check with the city at 505/984-6592 or at your hotel for route information. Santa Fe taxi service can be slow, particularly in the summer, but it's fine for an occasional excursion if you're relying primarily on your feet. Call Capital City Cab Company at 505/988-1211.

If you get to Santa Fe without a car and decide you want one, several of the national rental agencies have offices in the city. Two options downtown are Avis (505/982-4361), at the Desert Inn, and Hertz (505/982-1844), at the Hilton. Out on Cerrillos Road, try Budget (1946 Cerrillos, 505/984-8028) or Payless (3570 Cerrillos, 505/473-3189).

Visitor Information

The Santa Fe Convention and Visitor Bureau (201 W. Marcy, Santa Fe 87501, 800/528-5369 or 505/984-6760) provides a variety of free information and helps with questions. For current activities, obtain a copy of the "Pasatiempo" section of the local newspaper, the *New Mexican* (202 E. Marcy, Santa Fe 87501, 505/983-3303), for the Friday before your visit.

Footsteps Across New Mexico, in the Inn at Loretto (211 Old Santa Fe Trail, 505/982-9297), shows a short film about local history every 30 minutes from 9:30 to 5:00 year-round, in addition to selling books about New Mexico.

Other good places to browse for regional books are the museum shop of the Palace of the Governors, the newsstand at La Fonda Hotel, and three bookstores within a half-block of each other on West San Francisco: Collected Works at 208-B, Caxton Books at 216 and Santa Fe Bookseller at 203. Away from the plaza, check out Garcia Street Books (376 Garcia at Acequia Madre), Books West (Coronado Shopping Center on Cordova), and Old Santa Fe Bookstore (613 Old Santa Fe Trail). Used and rare books on the West are the specialties of Parker Books of the West (142 W. Palace) and Palace Avenue Books (209 E. Palace).

Guide Services

Discover Santa Fe (924 Paseo de Peralta, 505/982-4979), Santa Fe Detours (La Fonda Hotel, 505/983-6565), Rocky Mountain Tours (1323 Paseo de Peralta, 505/984-1684) and RojoTours (228 Old Santa Fe Trail, 505/983-8333) will cater to almost any visitor's whim, from booking rooms to leading customized expeditions. Southwest Adventure Group (505/983-0876) provides a different array of options including ghost tours of downtown.

Aboot and About in Santa Fe/Santa Fe Walks (Eldorado Hotel, 505/988-4455, ext. 108) offers a two-and-a-half-hour guided walking tour through historic areas of the city. It starts at the Eldorado Hotel twice daily and costs $10. Afoot in Santa Fe (Inn at Loretto, 505/983-3701) offers a walk of similar length and price from an office just behind the Inn at Loretto. The same folks operate the Loretto Line, an open-air jitney service, with a two-and-a-quarter-hour tour of downtown, Canyon Road and the scenic east side, with no stops, that costs $7. It leaves the Inn at Loretto parking lot three times daily, from midmorning to mid-afternoon. The Old Santa Fe Express, operated by Fiesta Tours (505/984-8235), traverses a similar course in a rushed one and a half hours. You can hop on four times a day at the corner of Palace Avenue and Lincoln Street, adjacent to the plaza, for $7.

If you don't want to mingle with the masses, Santa Fe HoteLimo (505/988-3535) escorts individuals or intimate groups around Santa Fe and northern New Mexico in spiffier transportation. Most folks request less-conspicuous Lincoln Town Cars but stretch limos are available if you want to pull out all the stops. The chauffeurs know the area well. A two-hour minimum at $30 per hour is required.

Other Services

Except where indicated, the area code is 505.

- *Automobile repairs*—Pep Boys, 2710 Cerrillos (473-3463)
- *Babysitting*—Kid Connection (471-3100)
- *Barber*—Cutting Edge, 120 E. Marcy (982-8135)
- *Beauty salon*—Inheritance Salons, 500 Montezuma in Sanbusco Center (988-3840) and La Fonda Hotel (986-8898)
- *Camera repairs*—Darkroom, 216 Galisteo (982-1502)
- *Dry cleaning, laundry, tailoring*—One Hour Martinizing, 200 E. Water (982-8606)
- *Fax and photocopying*—Kinko's, 333 Montezuma (982-6311)
- *Foreign currency exchange*—Sunwest Bank, main branch, 1234 St. Michael's (471-1234)
- *Film and one-hour film processing*—Fox Photo, 112 W. San Francisco (984-8307)
- *Groceries and liquor downtown*—Kaune's Specialties and Spirits, 208 Washington (983-7378)

◆ *Limousine*—Santa Fe HoteLimo (988-3535)
◆ *Mailing and packing*—Pak Mail, 369 Montezuma at Guadalupe, downtown (989-7280); AIM Mail Centers, 112 W. San Francisco in Plaza Mercado, downtown (982-5151)
◆ *Medical emergency*—Lovelace, 901 W. Alameda (982-3256); St. Vincent Hospital, 455 St. Michael's Drive (983-3361)
◆ *Messenger*—Pigeon Express Delivery (473-3447)
◆ *National/international courier*—Federal Express, Albuquerque (800/238-5355); Airborne Express, Albuquerque (842-4288)
◆ *Optical*—Quintana Optical, 109 E. Marcy (988-4234)
◆ *Pharmacy*—Fraser Pharmacy, 501 Old Santa Fe Trail (982-5524) for 24-hour emergency service
◆ *Police and other emergencies*—call 911; County Sheriff (986-6260)
◆ *Post office*—Downtown branch, South Federal (988-6351)
◆ *Radio news*—KTRC-AM 1400
◆ *Secretarial services*—Santa Fe Services, 142 Lincoln, Suite 205 (984-8511)
◆ *Shoe repairs*—Jacob's Shoe Repair Shop, 646 Old Santa Fe Trail (982-9774)
◆ *Travel accessories*—Le Bon Voyage, 328 S. Guadalupe (986-1260)
◆ *Western Union wire transfers*—Mail Boxes Etc. USA, 2442 Cerrillos (473-3020)

Climate and Clothing

Because of the altitude, Santa Fe's sun is intense and the air is cool. In the summer the sun begins to dominate the day about 10:00 A.M., but as soon as it disappears the mountain air whisks away the heat. Shorts are comfortable for six to ten hours a day; light sweaters or jackets are useful for the evening and early morning. The experienced take blankets or heavy coats for late nights at the opera. While the sun reigns during the day—frying a sunbather in half the time required at sea level—the humidity is always low, making the heat much less oppressive than in hazier cities to the north.

Winter days are cold and often snowy but seldom frozen over. Ski jackets or the equivalent are needed from at least November through March. The sun stays strong, however, and is considerably more effective at snow removal than the city's mechanical methods. Even in the depths of winter, Santa Fe remains the dancing ground of the sun.

Index